Algorithms Illuminated
Part 1: The Basics

Tim Roughgarden

First Edition

Third Printing, 2018

Cover image: *Stanza*, by Andrea Belag

ISBN: 978-0-9992829-0-8 (Paperback)
ISBN: 978-0-9992829-1-5 (ebook)

Library of Congress Control Number: 2017914282

Soundlikeyourself Publishing, LLC
San Francisco, CA
soundlikeyourselfpublishing@gmail.com
www.algorithmsilluminated.org

To Emma

Contents

Preface

This book is the first of a four-part series based on my online algorithms courses that have been running regularly since 2012, which in turn are based on an undergraduate course that I've taught many times at Stanford University.

What We'll Cover

Algorithms Illuminated, Part 1 provides an introduction to and basic literacy in the following four topics.

Asymptotic analysis and big-O notation. Asymptotic notation provides the basic vocabulary for discussing the design and analysis of algorithms. The key concept here is "big-O" notation, which is a modeling choice about the granularity with which we measure the running time of an algorithm. We'll see that the sweet spot for clear high-level thinking about algorithm design is to ignore constant factors and lower-order terms, and to concentrate on how an algorithm's performance scales with the size of the input.

Divide-and-conquer algorithms and the master method. There's no silver bullet in algorithm design, no single problem-solving method that cracks all computational problems. However, there are a few general algorithm design techniques that find successful application across a range of different domains. In this part of the series, we'll cover the "divide-and-conquer" technique. The idea is to break a problem into smaller subproblems, solve the subproblems recursively, and then quickly combine their solutions into one for the original problem. We'll see fast divide-and-conquer algorithms for sorting, integer and matrix multiplication, and a basic problem in computational geometry. We'll also cover the master method, which is a powerful tool for analyzing the running time of divide-and-conquer algorithms.

Randomized algorithms. A randomized algorithm "flips coins" as it runs, and its behavior can depend on the outcomes of these coin flips. Surprisingly often, randomization leads to simple, elegant, and practical algorithms. The canonical example is randomized QuickSort, and we'll explain this algorithm and its running time analysis in detail.

Sorting and selection. As a byproduct of studying the first three topics, we'll learn several famous algorithms for sorting and selection, including MergeSort, QuickSort, and linear-time selection (both randomized and deterministic). These computational primitives are so blazingly fast that they do not take much more time than that needed just to read the input. It's important to cultivate a collection of such "for-free primitives," both to apply directly to data and to use as the building blocks for solutions to more difficult problems.

For a more detailed look into the book's contents, check out the "Upshot" sections that conclude each chapter and highlight the most important points.

Topics covered in the other three parts. *Algorithms Illuminated, Part 2* covers data structures (heaps, balanced search trees, hash tables, bloom filters), graph primitives (breadth- and depth-first search, connectivity, shortest paths), and their applications (ranging from deduplication to social network analysis). *Part 3* focuses on greedy algorithms (scheduling, minimum spanning trees, clustering, Huffman codes) and dynamic programming (knapsack, sequence alignment, shortest paths, optimal search trees). *Part 4* is all about NP-completeness, what it means for the algorithm designer, and strategies for coping with computationally intractable problems, including the analysis of heuristics and local search.

Skills You'll Learn

Mastering algorithms takes time and effort. Why bother?

Become a better programmer. You'll learn several blazingly fast subroutines for processing data as well as several useful data structures for organizing data that you can deploy directly in your own programs. Implementing and using these algorithms will stretch and improve your programming skills. You'll also learn general algorithm design paradigms that are relevant for many different problems across different domains, as well as tools for predicting the performance of such algorithms. These "algorithmic design patterns" can help you come up with new algorithms for problems that arise in your own work.

Sharpen your analytical skills. You'll get lots of practice describing and reasoning about algorithms. Through mathematical analysis, you'll gain a deep understanding of the specific algorithms and data structures covered in these books. You'll acquire facility with several mathematical techniques that are broadly useful for analyzing algorithms.

Think algorithmically. After you learn about algorithms it's hard not to see them everywhere, whether you're riding an elevator, watching a flock of birds, managing your investment portfolio, or even watching an infant learn. Algorithmic thinking is increasingly useful and prevalent in disciplines outside of computer science, including biology, statistics, and economics.

Literacy with computer science's greatest hits. Studying algorithms can feel like watching a highlight reel of many of the greatest hits from the last sixty years of computer science. No longer will you feel excluded at that computer science cocktail party when someone cracks a joke about Dijkstra's algorithm. After reading these books, you'll know exactly what they mean.

Ace your technical interviews. Over the years, countless students have regaled me with stories about how mastering the concepts in these books enabled them to ace every technical interview question they were ever asked.

How These Books Are Different

This series of books has only one goal: *to teach the basics of algorithms in the most accessible way possible.* Think of them as a transcript of what an expert algorithms tutor would say to you over a series of one-on-one lessons.

There are a number of excellent more traditional and encyclopedic textbooks on algorithms, any of which usefully complement this book series with additional details, problems, and topics. I encourage you to explore and find your own favorites. There are also several books that, unlike these books, cater to programmers looking for ready-made algorithm implementations in a specific programming language. Many such implementations are freely available on the Web as well.

Who Are You?

The whole point of these books and the online courses upon which they are based is to be as widely and easily accessible as possible. People of all ages, backgrounds, and walks of life are well represented in my online courses, and there are large numbers of students (high-school, college, etc.), software engineers (both current and aspiring), scientists, and professionals hailing from all corners of the world.

This book is not an introduction to programming, and ideally you've acquired basic programming skills in a standard language (like Java, Python, C, Scala, Haskell, etc.). For a litmus test, check out Section 1.4—if it makes sense, you'll be fine for the rest of the book. If you need to beef up your programming skills, there are several outstanding free online courses that teach basic programming.

We also use mathematical analysis as needed to understand how and why algorithms really work. The freely available book *Mathematics for Computer Science*, by Eric Lehman, F. Thomson Leighton, and Albert R. Meyer is an excellent and entertaining refresher on mathematical notation (like $\sum$ and $\forall$), the basics of proofs (induction, contradiction, etc.), discrete probability, and much more. Appendices A and B also provide quick reviews of proofs by induction and discrete probability, respectively. The starred sections are the most mathematically intense ones. The math-phobic or time-constrained reader can skip these on a first reading without loss of continuity.

Additional Resources

These books are based on online courses that are currently running on the Coursera and Stanford Lagunita platforms. I've made several resources available to help you replicate as much of the online course experience as you like.

Videos. If you're more in the mood to watch and listen than to read, check out the YouTube video playlists available from www.algorithmsilluminated.org. These videos cover all of the topics of this book series. I hope they exude a contagious enthusiasm for algorithms that, alas, is impossible to replicate fully on the printed page.

Quizzes. How can you know if you're truly absorbing the concepts in this book? Quizzes with solutions and explanations are scattered throughout the text; when you encounter one, I encourage you to pause and think about the answer before reading on.

End-of-chapter problems. At the end of each chapter you'll find several relatively straightforward questions for testing your understanding, followed by harder and more open-ended challenge problems. Solutions to problems that are marked with an "*(S)*" appear at the end of the book. Readers can interact with me and each other about the remaining end-of-chapter problems through the book's discussion forums (see below).

Programming problems. Many of the chapters conclude with a suggested programming project, whose goal is to help you develop a detailed understanding of an algorithm by creating your own working implementation of it. Data sets, along with test cases and their solutions, can be found at www.algorithmsilluminated.org.

Discussion forums. A big reason for the success of online courses is the opportunities they provide for participants to help each other understand the course material and debug programs through discussion forums. Readers of these books have the same opportunity, via the forums available at www.algorithmsilluminated.org.

Acknowledgments

These books would not exist without the passion and hunger supplied by the hundreds of thousands of participants in my algorithms courses over the years, both on campus at Stanford and on online platforms. I am particularly grateful to those who supplied detailed feedback on an earlier draft of this book: Tonya Blust, Yuan Cao, Jim Humelsine, Bayram Kuliyev, Patrick Monkelban, Kyle Schiller, Nissanka Wickremasinghe, and Daniel Zingaro.

I always appreciate suggestions and corrections from readers. These are best communicated through the discussion forums mentioned above.

Tim Roughgarden
Stanford, California
September 2017

Chapter 1

Introduction

The goal of this chapter is to get you excited about the study of algorithms. We begin by discussing algorithms in general and why they're so important. Then we use the problem of multiplying two integers to illustrate how algorithmic ingenuity can improve on more straightforward or naive solutions. We then discuss the `MergeSort` algorithm in detail, for several reasons: it's a practical and famous algorithm that you should know; it's a good warm-up to get you ready for more intricate algorithms; and it's the canonical introduction to the "divide-and-conquer" algorithm design paradigm. The chapter concludes by describing several guiding principles for how we'll analyze algorithms throughout the rest of the book.

1.1 Why Study Algorithms?

Let me begin by justifying this book's existence and giving you some reasons why you should be highly motivated to learn about algorithms. So what is an algorithm, anyway? It's a set of well-defined rules—a recipe, in effect—for solving some computational problem. Maybe you have a bunch of numbers and you want to rearrange them so that they're in sorted order. Maybe you have a road map and you want to compute the shortest path from some origin to some destination. Maybe you need to complete several tasks before certain deadlines, and you want to know in what order you should finish the tasks so that you complete them all by their respective deadlines.

So why study algorithms?

Important for all other branches of computer science. First, understanding the basics of algorithms and the closely related field of data structures is essential for doing serious work in pretty much any branch of computer science. For example, at Stanford University, every degree the computer science department offers (B.S., M.S., and Ph.D.) requires an algorithms course. To name just a few examples:

1. Routing protocols in communication networks piggyback on classical shortest path algorithms.

2. Public-key cryptography relies on efficient number-theoretic algorithms.

3. Computer graphics requires the computational primitives supplied by geometric algorithms.

4. Database indices rely on balanced search tree data structures.

5. Computational biology uses dynamic programming algorithms to measure genome similarity.

And the list goes on.

Driver of technological innovation. Second, algorithms play a key role in modern technological innovation. To give just one obvious example, search engines use a tapestry of algorithms to efficiently compute the relevance of various Web pages to a given search query. The most famous such algorithm is the `PageRank` algorithm currently in use by Google. Indeed, in a December 2010 report to the United States White House, the President's council of advisers on science and technology wrote the following:

> "Everyone knows Moore's Law — a prediction made in 1965 by Intel co-founder Gordon Moore that the density of transistors in integrated circuits would continue to double every 1 to 2 years... in many areas, performance gains due to improvements in algorithms have vastly exceeded even the dramatic performance gains due to increased processor speed."[1]

---

[1]Excerpt from Report to the President and Congress: Designing a Digital Future, December 2010 (page 71).

Lens on other sciences. Third, although this is beyond the scope of this book, algorithms are increasingly used to provide a novel "lens" on processes outside of computer science and technology. For example, the study of quantum computation has provided a new computational viewpoint on quantum mechanics. Price fluctuations in economic markets can be fruitfully viewed as an algorithmic process. Even evolution can be thought of as a surprisingly effective search algorithm.

Good for the brain. Back when I was a student, my favorite classes were always the challenging ones that, after I struggled through them, left me feeling a few IQ points smarter than when I started. I hope this material provides a similar experience for you.

Fun! Finally, I hope that by the end of the book you can see why the design and analysis of algorithms is simply fun. It's an endeavor that requires a rare blend of precision and creativity. It can certainly be frustrating at times, but it's also highly addictive. And let's not forget that you've been learning about algorithms since you were a little kid.

1.2   Integer Multiplication

1.2.1   Problems and Solutions

When you were in third grade or so, you probably learned an algorithm for multiplying two numbers—a well-defined set of rules for transforming an input (two numbers) into an output (their product). It's important to distinguish between two different things: the description of the *problem being solved*, and that of the *method of solution* (that is, the algorithm for the problem). In this book, we'll repeatedly follow the pattern of first introducing a computational problem (the inputs and desired output), and then describing one or more algorithms that solve the problem.

1.2.2   The Integer Multiplication Problem

In the integer multiplication problem, the input is two n-digit numbers, which we'll call x and y. The length n of x and y could be any positive integer, but I encourage you to think of n as large, in the thousands or even more.[2] (Perhaps you're implementing a cryptographic application that must manipulate very large numbers.) The desired output in the integer multiplication problem is just the product $x \cdot y$.

Problem: Integer Multiplication

Input: Two n-digit nonnegative integers, x and y.

Output: The product $x \cdot y$.

1.2.3 The Grade-School Algorithm

Having defined the computational problem precisely, we describe an algorithm that solves it—the same algorithm you learned in third grade. We will assess the performance of this algorithm through the number of "primitive operations" it performs, as a function of the number of digits n in each input number. For now, let's think of a primitive operation as any of the following: (i) adding two single-digit numbers; (ii) multiplying two single-digit numbers; or (iii) adding a zero to the beginning or end of a number.

To jog your memory, consider the concrete example of multiplying $x = 5678$ and $y = 1234$ (so $n = 4$). See also Figure 1.1. The algorithm first computes the "partial product" of the first number and the last digit of the second number $5678 \cdot 4 = 22712$. Computing this partial product boils down to multiplying each of the digits of the first number by 4, and adding in "carries" as necessary.[3] When computing the next partial product ($5678 \cdot 3 = 17034$), we do the same thing, shifting the result one digit to the left, effectively adding a "0" at the end. And so on for the final two partial products. The final step is to add up all the partial products.

Back in third grade, you probably accepted that this algorithm is *correct*, meaning that no matter what numbers x and y you start with, provided that all intermediate computations are done properly, it eventually terminates with the product $x \cdot y$ of the two input numbers.

---

[2]If you want to multiply numbers with different lengths (like 1234 and 56), a simple hack is to just add some zeros to the beginning of the smaller number (for example, treat 56 as 0056). Alternatively, the algorithms we'll discuss can be modified to accommodate numbers with different lengths.

[3]$8 \cdot 4 = 32$, carry the 3, $7 \cdot 4 = 28$, plus 3 is 31, carry the 3, ...

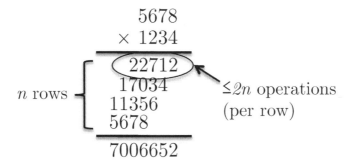

Figure 1.1: The grade-school integer multiplication algorithm.

That is, you're never going to get a wrong answer, and the algorithm can't loop forever.

1.2.4   Analysis of the Number of Operations

Your third-grade teacher might not have discussed the number of primitive operations needed to carry out this procedure to its conclusion. To compute the first partial product, we multiplied 4 times each of the digits $5, 6, 7, 8$ of the first number. This is 4 primitive operations. We also performed a few additions because of the carries. In general, computing a partial product involves n multiplications (one per digit) and at most n additions (at most one per digit), for a total of at most $2n$ primitive operations. There's nothing special about the first partial product: every partial product requires at most $2n$ operations. Since there are n partial products—one per digit of the second number—computing all of them requires at most $n \cdot 2n = 2n^2$ primitive operations. We still have to add them all up to compute the final answer, but this takes a comparable number of operations (at most another $2n^2$). Summarizing:

$$\textbf{total number of operations} \leq \underbrace{\textbf{constant}}_{=4} \cdot \textbf{n}^2.$$

Thinking about how the amount of work the algorithm performs *scales* as the input numbers grow bigger and bigger, we see that the work required grows quadratically with the number of digits. If you double the length of the input numbers, the work required jumps by a factor of 4. Quadruple their length and it jumps by a factor of 16, and so on.

1.2.5   Can We Do Better?

Depending on what type of third-grader you were, you might well have accepted this procedure as the unique or at least optimal way to multiply two numbers. If you want to be a serious algorithm designer, you'll need to grow out of that kind of obedient timidity. The classic algorithms book by Aho, Hopcroft, and Ullman, after iterating through a number of algorithm design paradigms, has this to say:

> "Perhaps the most important principle for the good algorithm designer is to refuse to be content."[4]

Or as I like to put it, every algorithm designer should adopt the mantra:

> *Can we do better?*

This question is particularly apropos when you're faced with a naive or straightforward solution to a computational problem. In the third grade, you might not have asked if one could do better than the straightforward integer multiplication algorithm. Now is the time to ask, and answer, this question.

1.3   Karatsuba Multiplication

The algorithm design space is surprisingly rich, and there are certainly other interesting methods of multiplying two integers beyond what you learned in the third grade. This section describes a method called *Karatsuba multiplication*.[5]

---

[4]Alfred V. Aho, John E. Hopcroft, and Jeffrey D. Ullman, *The Design and Analysis of Computer Algorithms*, Addison-Wesley, 1974, page 70.

[5]Discovered in 1960 by Anatoly Karatsuba, who at the time was a 23-year-old student.

1.3.1   A Concrete Example

To get a feel for Karatsuba multiplication, let's re-use our previous example with $x = 5678$ and $y = 1234$. We're going to execute a sequence of steps, quite different from the grade-school algorithm, culminating in the product $x \cdot y$. The sequence of steps should strike you as very mysterious, like pulling a rabbit out of a hat; later in the section we'll explain exactly what Karatsuba multiplication is and why it works. The key point to appreciate now is that there's a dazzling array of options for solving computational problems like integer multiplication.

First, to regard the first and second halves of x as numbers in their own right, we give them the names a and b (so $a = 56$ and $b = 78$). Similarly, c and d denote 12 and 34, respectively (Figure 1.2).

Figure 1.2: Thinking of 4-digit numbers as pairs of double-digit numbers.

Next we'll perform a sequence of operations that involve only the double-digit numbers a, b, c, and d, and finally collect all the terms together in a magical way that results in the product of x and y.

Step 1: Compute $a \cdot c = 56 \cdot 12$, which is 672 (as you're welcome to check).

Step 2: Compute $b \cdot d = 78 \cdot 34 = 2652$.

The next two steps are still more inscrutable.

Step 3: Compute $(a + b) \cdot (c + d) = 134 \cdot 46 = 6164$.

Step 4: Subtract the results of the first two steps from the result of the third step: $6164 - 672 - 2652 = 2840$.

Finally, we add up the results of steps 1, 2, and 4, but only after adding four trailing zeroes to the answer in step 1 and 2 trailing zeroes to the answer in step 4.

Step 5: Compute $10^4 \cdot 672 + 10^2 \cdot 2840 + 2652 = 6720000 + 284000 + 2652 = 7006652$.

This is exactly the same (correct) result computed by the grade-school algorithm in Section 1.2!

You should not have any intuition about what just happened. Rather, I hope that you feel some mixture of bafflement and intrigue, and appreciate the fact that there seem to be fundamentally different algorithms for multiplying integers than the one you learned as a kid. Once you realize how rich the space of algorithms is, you have to wonder: can we do better than the third-grade algorithm? Does the algorithm above already do better?

1.3.2   A Recursive Algorithm

Before tackling full-blown Karatsuba multiplication, let's explore a simpler recursive approach to integer multiplication.[6] A recursive algorithm for integer multiplication presumably involves multiplications of numbers with fewer digits (like 12, 34, 56, and 78 in the computation above).

In general, a number x with an even number n of digits can be expressed in terms of two $n/2$-digit numbers, its first half and second half a and b:

$$x = 10^{n/2} \cdot a + b.$$

Similarly, we can write

$$y = 10^{n/2} \cdot c + d.$$

To compute the product of x and y, let's use the two expressions above and multiply out:

$$x \cdot y = (10^{n/2} \cdot a + b) \cdot (10^{n/2} \cdot c + d)$$
$$= 10^n \cdot (a \cdot c) + 10^{n/2} \cdot (a \cdot d + b \cdot c) + b \cdot d. \qquad (1.1)$$

---

[6]I'm assuming you've heard of recursion as part of your programming background. A recursive procedure is one that invokes itself as a subroutine with a smaller input, until a base case is reached.

Note that all of the multiplications in (1.1) are either between pairs of $n/2$-digit numbers or involve a power of 10.[7]

The expression (1.1) suggests a recursive approach to multiplying two numbers. To compute the product $x \cdot y$, we compute the expression (1.1). The four relevant products ($a \cdot c$, $a \cdot d$, $b \cdot c$, and $b \cdot d$) all concern numbers with fewer than n digits, so we can compute each of them recursively. Once our four recursive calls come back to us with their answers, we can compute the expression (1.1) in the obvious way: tack on n trailing zeroes to $a \cdot c$, add $a \cdot d$ and $b \cdot c$ (using grade-school addition) and tack on $n/2$ trailing zeroes to the result, and finally add these two expressions to $b \cdot d$.[8] We summarize this algorithm, which we'll call RecIntMult, in the following pseudocode.[9]

RecIntMult

Input: two n-digit positive integers x and y.
Output: the product $x \cdot y$.
Assumption: n is a power of 2.

---

if $n = 1$ then   // base case
    compute $x \cdot y$ in one step and return the result
else   // recursive case
    $a, b :=$ first and second halves of x
    $c, d :=$ first and second halves of y
    recursively compute $ac := a \cdot c$, $ad := a \cdot d$,
      $bc := b \cdot c$, and $bd := b \cdot d$
    compute $10^n \cdot ac + 10^{n/2} \cdot (ad + bc) + bd$ using
      grade-school addition and return the result

Is the RecIntMult algorithm faster or slower than the grade-school

---

[7]For simplicity, we are assuming that n is a power of 2. A simple hack for enforcing this assumption is to add an appropriate number of leading zeroes to x and y, which at most doubles their lengths. Alternatively, when n is odd, it's also fine to break x and y into two numbers with almost equal lengths.

[8]Recursive algorithms also need one or more base cases, so that they don't keep calling themselves until the rest of time. Here, the base case is: if x and y are 1-digit numbers, just multiply them in one primitive operation and return the result.

[9]In pseudocode, we use "=" to denote an equality test, and ":=" to denote a variable assignment.

algorithm? You shouldn't necessarily have any intuition about this question, and the answer will have to wait until Chapter 4.

1.3.3   Karatsuba Multiplication

Karatsuba multiplication is an optimized version of the `RecIntMult` algorithm. We again start from the expansion (1.1) of $x \cdot y$ in terms of a, b, c, and d. The `RecIntMult` algorithm uses four recursive calls, one for each of the products in (1.1) between $n/2$-digit numbers. But we don't really care about $a \cdot d$ or $b \cdot c$, except inasmuch as we care about their sum $a \cdot d + b \cdot c$. With only three quantities that we care about—$a \cdot c$, $a \cdot d + b \cdot c$, and $b \cdot d$—can we get away with only three recursive calls?

To see that we can, first use two recursive calls to compute $a \cdot c$ and $b \cdot d$, as before.

Step 1:   Recursively compute $a \cdot c$.

Step 2:   Recursively compute $b \cdot d$.

Instead of recursively computing $a \cdot d$ or $b \cdot c$, we recursively compute the product of $a + b$ and $c + d$.[10]

Step 3:   Compute $a + b$ and $c + d$ (using grade-school addition), and recursively compute $(a + b) \cdot (c + d)$.

The key trick in Karatsuba multiplication goes back to the early 19th-century mathematician Carl Friedrich Gauss, who was thinking about multiplying complex numbers. Subtracting the results of the first two steps from the result of the third step gives exactly what we want, the middle coefficient in (1.1) of $a \cdot d + b \cdot c$:

$$\underbrace{(a + b) \cdot (c + d)}_{=\, a\cdot c + a\cdot d + b\cdot c + b\cdot d} -\, a \cdot c - b \cdot d = a \cdot d + b \cdot c.$$

Step 4:   Subtract the results of the first two steps from the result of the third step to obtain $a \cdot d + b \cdot c$.

The final step computes (1.1), as in the `RecIntMult` algorithm.

---

[10]The numbers $a + b$ and $c + d$ might have as many as $(n/2) + 1$ digits, but the algorithm still works fine.

Step 5: Compute (1.1) by adding up the results of steps 1, 2, and 4, after adding 10^n trailing zeroes to the answer in step 1 and $10^{n/2}$ trailing zeroes to the answer in step 4.

Karatsuba

Input: two n-digit positive integers x and y.
Output: the product $x \cdot y$.
Assumption: n is a power of 2.

---

if $n = 1$ **then**   `// base case`
    compute $x \cdot y$ in one step and return the result
else   `// recursive case`
    $a, b :=$ first and second halves of x
    $c, d :=$ first and second halves of y
    compute $p := a + b$ and $q := c + d$ using
      grade-school addition
    recursively compute $ac := a \cdot c$, $bd := b \cdot d$, and
      $pq := p \cdot q$
    compute $adbc := pq - ac - bd$ using grade-school
      addition
    compute $10^n \cdot ac + 10^{n/2} \cdot adbc + bd$ using
      grade-school addition and return the result

Thus Karatsuba multiplication makes only three recursive calls! Saving a recursive call should save on the overall running time, but by how much? Is the `Karatsuba` algorithm faster than the grade-school multiplication algorithm? The answer is far from obvious, but it is an easy application of the tools you'll acquire in Chapter 4 for analyzing the running time of such "divide-and-conquer" algorithms.

On Pseudocode

This book explains algorithms using a mixture of high-level pseudocode and English (as in this section). I'm assuming that you have the skills to translate such high-level descriptions into working code in your favorite programming language. Several other books

and resources on the Web offer concrete implementations of various algorithms in specific programming
languages.

The first benefit of emphasizing high-level descriptions over language-specific implementations is flexi-
bility: while I assume familiarity with *some* programming language, I don't care which one. Second, this
approach promotes the understanding of algorithms
at a deep and conceptual level, unencumbered by low-
level details. Seasoned programmers and computer
scientists generally think and communicate about algorithms at a similarly high level.

Still, there is no substitute for the detailed understanding of an algorithm that comes from providing
your own working implementation of it. I strongly
encourage you to implement as many of the algorithms in this book as you have time for. (It's also a
great excuse to pick up a new programming language!)
For guidance, see the end-of-chapter Programming
Problems and supporting test cases.

1.4   MergeSort: The Algorithm

This section provides our first taste of analyzing the running time of
a non-trivial algorithm—the famous MergeSort algorithm.

1.4.1   Motivation

MergeSort is a relatively ancient algorithm, and was certainly known
to John von Neumann as early as 1945. Why begin a modern course
on algorithms with such an old example?

Oldie but a goodie.   Despite being over 70 years old, MergeSort
is still one of the methods of choice for sorting. It's used all the time
in practice, and is the standard sorting algorithm in a number of
programming libraries.

Canonical divide-and-conquer algorithm. The "divide-and-conquer" algorithm design paradigm is a general approach to solving problems, with applications in many different domains. The basic idea is to break your problem into smaller subproblems, solve the subproblems recursively, and finally combine the solutions to the subproblems into one for the original problem. MergeSort is an ideal introduction to the divide-and-conquer paradigm, the benefits it offers, and the analysis challenges it presents.

Calibrate your preparation. Our MergeSort discussion will give you a good indication of whether your current skill set is a good match for this book. My assumption is that you have the programming and mathematical backgrounds to (with some work) translate the high-level idea of MergeSort into a working program in your favorite programming language and to follow our running time analysis of the algorithm. If this and the next section make sense, then you are in good shape for the rest of the book.

Motivates guiding principles for algorithm analysis. Our running time analysis of MergeSort exposes a number of more general guiding principles, such as the quest for running time bounds that hold for every input of a given size, and the importance of the rate of growth of an algorithm's running time (as a function of the input size).

Warm-up for the master method. We'll analyze MergeSort using the "recursion tree method," which is a way of tallying up the operations performed by a recursive algorithm. Chapter 4 builds on these ideas and culminates with the "master method," a powerful and easy-to-use tool for bounding the running time of many different divide-and-conquer algorithms, including the RecIntMult and Karatsuba algorithms of Section 1.3.

1.4.2   Sorting

You probably already know the sorting problem and some algorithms that solve it, but just so we're all on the same page:

Problem: Sorting

Input: An array of n numbers, in arbitrary order.

Output: An array of the same numbers, sorted from smallest to largest.

For example, given the input array

5	4	1	8	7	2	6	3

the desired output array is

1	2	3	4	5	6	7	8

In the example above, the eight numbers in the input array are distinct. Sorting isn't really any harder when there are duplicates, and it can even be easier. But to keep the discussion as simple as possible, let's assume—among friends—that the numbers in the input array are always distinct. I strongly encourage you to think about how our sorting algorithms need to be modified (if at all) to handle duplicates.[11]

If you don't care about optimizing the running time, it's not too difficult to come up with a correct sorting algorithm. Perhaps the simplest approach is to first scan through the input array to identify the minimum element and copy it over to the first element of the output array; then do another scan to identify and copy over the second-smallest element; and so on. This algorithm is called `SelectionSort`. You may have heard of `InsertionSort`, which can be viewed as a slicker implementation of the same idea of iteratively growing a prefix of the sorted output array. You might also know `BubbleSort`, in which you identify adjacent pairs of elements that

---

[11]In practice, there is often data (called the *value*) associated with each number (which is called the *key*). For example, you might want to sort employee records (with the name, salary, etc.), using social security numbers as keys. We focus on sorting the keys, with the understanding that each key retains its associated data.

are out of order, and perform repeated swaps until the entire array is sorted. All of these algorithms have quadratic running times, meaning that the number of operations performed on arrays of length n scales with n^2, the square of the input length. Can we do better? By using the divide-and-conquer paradigm, the MergeSort algorithm improves dramatically over these more straightforward sorting algorithms.[12]

1.4.3   An Example

The easiest way to understand MergeSort is through a picture of a concrete example (Figure 1.3). We'll use the input array from Section 1.4.2.

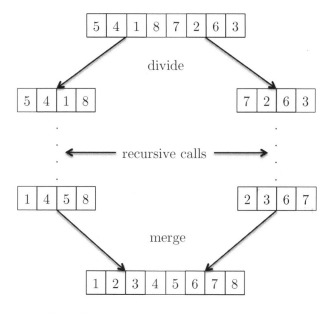

Figure 1.3: A bird's-eye view of MergeSort on a concrete example.

As a recursive divide-and-conquer algorithm, MergeSort calls itself on smaller arrays. The simplest way to decompose a sorting problem into smaller sorting problems is to break the input array in half. The first and second halves are each sorted recursively. For example, in

---

[12]While generally dominated by MergeSort, InsertionSort is still useful in practice in certain cases, especially for small input sizes.

Figure 1.3, the first and second halves of the input array are $\{5, 4, 1, 8\}$ and $\{7, 2, 6, 3\}$. By the magic of recursion (or induction, if you prefer), the first recursive call correctly sorts the first half, returning the array $\{1, 4, 5, 8\}$. The second recursive call returns the array $\{2, 3, 6, 7\}$. The final "merge" step combines these two sorted arrays of length 4 into a single sorted array of all 8 numbers. Details of this step are given below, but the idea is to walk indices down each of the sorted subarrays, populating the output array from left to right in sorted order.

1.4.4   Pseudocode

The picture in Figure 1.3 suggests the following pseudocode, with two recursive calls and a merge step, for the general problem. As usual, our description cannot necessarily be translated line by line into working code (though it's pretty close).

MergeSort

Input: array A of n distinct integers.
Output: array with the same integers, sorted from
  smallest to largest.

```
// ignoring base cases
```
$C :=$ recursively sort first half of A
$D :=$ recursively sort second half of A
return **Merge** (C,D)

There are several omissions from the pseudocode that deserve comment. As a recursive algorithm, there should also be one or more base cases, where there is no further recursion and the answer is returned directly. So if the input array A contains only 0 or 1 elements, **MergeSort** returns it (it is already sorted). The pseudocode does not detail what "first half" and "second half" mean when n is odd, but the obvious interpretation (with one "half" having one more element than the other) works fine. Finally, the pseudocode ignores the implementation details of how to actually pass the two subarrays to their respective recursive calls. These details depend somewhat on the programming language. The point of high-level pseudocode is to ignore such details and focus on the concepts that transcend any particular programming language.

1.4.5   The Merge Subroutine

How should we implement the Merge step? At this point, the two recursive calls have done their work and we have in our possession two sorted subarrays C and D of length $n/2$. The idea is to traverse both the sorted subarrays in order and populate the output array from left to right in sorted order.[13]

Merge

Input: sorted arrays C and D (length $n/2$ each).
Output: sorted array B (length n).
Simplifying assumption: n is even.

---

1 $i := 1$
2 $j := 1$
3 **for** $k := 1$ to n **do**
4   **if** $C[i] < D[j]$ **then**
5          $B[k] := C[i]$ // populate output array
6          $i := i + 1$ // increment i
7   **else**   // $D[j] < C[i]$
8          $B[k] := D[j]$
9          $j := j + 1$

We traverse the output array using the index k, and the sorted subarrays with the indices i and j. All three arrays are traversed from left to right. The for loop in line 3 implements the pass over the output array. In the first iteration, the subroutine identifies the minimum element in either C or D and copies it over to the first position of the output array B. The minimum element overall is either in C (in which case it's $C[1]$, since C is sorted) or in D (in which case it's $D[1]$, since D is sorted). Advancing the appropriate index (i or j)

---

[13]We number our array entries beginning with 1 (rather than 0), and use the syntax "$A[i]$" for the ith entry of an array A. These details vary across programming languages.

effectively removes from further consideration the element just copied, and the process is then repeated to identify the smallest element remaining in C or D (the second-smallest overall). In general, the smallest element not yet copied over to B is either $C[i]$ or $D[j]$; the subroutine explicitly checks to see which one is smaller and proceeds accordingly. Since every iteration copies over the smallest element still under consideration in C or D, the output array is indeed populated in sorted order.

As usual, our pseudocode is intentionally a bit sloppy, to emphasize the forest over the trees. A full implementation should also keep track of when the traversal of C or D falls off the end, at which point the remaining elements of the other array are copied into the final entries of B (in order). Now is a good time to work through your own implementation of the `MergeSort` algorithm.

1.5 MergeSort: The Analysis

What's the running time of the `MergeSort` algorithm, as a function of the length n of the input array? Is it faster than more straightforward methods of sorting, such as `SelectionSort`, `InsertionSort`, and `BubbleSort`? By "running time," we mean the number of lines of code executed in a concrete implementation of the algorithm. Think of walking line by line through this implementation using a debugger, one "primitive operation" at a time. We're interested in the number of steps the debugger takes before the program completes.

1.5.1 Running Time of Merge

Analyzing the running time of the `MergeSort` algorithm is an intimidating task, as it's a recursive algorithm that calls itself over and over. So let's warm up with the simpler task of understanding the number of operations performed by a single invocation of the `Merge` subroutine when called on two sorted arrays of length $\ell/2$ each. We can do this directly, by inspecting the code in Section 1.4.5 (where n corresponds to ℓ). First, lines 1 and 2 each perform an initialization, and we'll count this as two operations. Then, we have a for loop that executes a total of ℓ times. Each iteration of the loop performs a comparison in line 4, an assignment in either line 5 or line 8, and an increment in either line 6 or line 9. The loop index k also needs to get incremented each loop iteration. This means that 4 primitive operations are performed for each of the ℓ iterations of the loop.[14] Totaling up, we conclude that the Merge subroutine performs at most $4\ell + 2$ operations to merge two sorted arrays of length $\ell/2$ each. Let me abuse our friendship further with a true but sloppy inequality that will make our lives easier: for $\ell \geq 1$, $4\ell + 2 \leq 6\ell$. That is, 6ℓ is also a valid upper bound on the number of operations performed by the Merge subroutine.

Lemma 1.1 (Running Time of Merge) *For every pair of sorted input arrays C, D of length $\ell/2$, the Merge subroutine performs at most 6ℓ operations.*

On Lemmas, Theorems, and the Like

In mathematical writing, the most important technical statements are labeled *theorems*. A *lemma* is a technical statement that assists with the proof of a theorem (much as Merge assists with the implementation of MergeSort). A *corollary* is a statement that follows immediately from an already-proved result, such as a special case of a theorem. We use the term *proposition* for stand-alone technical statements that are not particularly important in their own right.

1.5.2 Running Time of MergeSort

How can we go from the straightforward analysis of the Merge subroutine to an analysis of MergeSort, a recursive algorithm that spawns further invocations of itself? Especially terrifying is the rapid proliferation of recursive calls, the number of which is blowing up exponentially with the depth of the recursion. The one thing we have going for us is the fact that every recursive call is passed an input substantially smaller than the one we started with. There's a tension between two

---

[14]One could quibble with the choice of 4. Does comparing the loop index k to its upper bound also count as an additional operation each iteration, for a total of 5? Section 1.6 explains why such differences in accounting don't really matter. So let's agree, among friends, that it's 4 primitive operations per iteration.

competing forces: on the one hand, the explosion of different subproblems that need to be solved; and on the other, the ever-shrinking
inputs for which these subproblems are responsible. Reconciling these
two forces will drive our analysis of MergeSort. In the end, we'll
prove the following concrete and useful upper bound on the number
of operations performed by MergeSort (across all its recursive calls).

Theorem 1.2 (Running Time of MergeSort**)** *For every input array of length $n \geq 1$, the* MergeSort *algorithm performs at most*

$$6n \log_2 n + 6n$$

operations, where $\log_2$ denotes the base-2 logarithm.

On Logarithms

Some students are unnecessarily frightened by the
appearance of a logarithm, which is actually a very
down-to-earth concept. For a positive integer n, $\log_2 n$
just means the following: type n into a calculator,
and count the number of times you need to divide it
by 2 before the result is 1 or less.[a] For example, it
takes five divide-by-twos to bring 32 down to 1, so
$\log_2 32 = 5$. Ten divide-by-twos bring 1024 down to 1,
so $\log_2 1024 = 10$. These examples make it intuitively
clear that $\log_2 n$ is much less than n (compare 10 vs.
1024), especially as n grows large. A plot confirms
this intuition (Figure 1.4).

---

[a]To be pedantic, $\log_2 n$ is not an integer if n is not a power
of 2, and what we have described is really $\log_2 n$ rounded up
to the nearest integer. We can ignore this minor distinction.

Theorem 1.2 is a win for the MergeSort algorithm and showcases
the benefits of the divide-and-conquer algorithm design paradigm. We
mentioned that the running times of simpler sorting algorithms, like
SelectionSort, InsertionSort, and BubbleSort, depend *quadratically* on the input size n, meaning that the number of operations
required scales as a constant times n^2. In Theorem 1.2, one of these

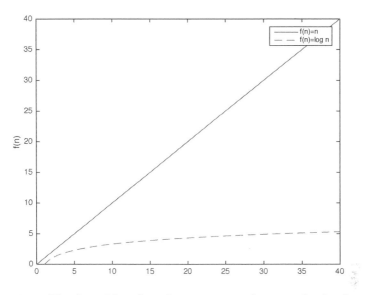

Figure 1.4: The logarithm function grows much more slowly than the identity function. The base of the logarithm is 2; other bases lead to qualitatively similar pictures.

factors of n is replaced by $\log_2 n$. As suggested by Figure 1.4, this means that MergeSort typically runs much faster than the simpler sorting algorithms, especially as n grows large.[15]

1.5.3   Proof of Theorem 1.2

We now do a full running time analysis of MergeSort, thereby substantiating the claim that a recursive divide-and-conquer approach results in a faster sorting algorithm than more straightforward methods. For simplicity, we assume that the input array length n is a power of 2. This assumption can be removed with minor additional work.

The plan for proving the running time bound in Theorem 1.2 is to use a *recursion tree*; see Figure 1.5.[16] The idea of the recursion tree method is to write out all the work done by a recursive algorithm in a tree structure, with nodes of the tree corresponding to recursive calls, and the children of a node corresponding to the recursive calls made

---

[15]See Section 1.6.3 for further discussion of this point.

[16]For some reason, computer scientists seem to think that trees grow downward.

by that node. This tree structure provides us with a principled way to
tally up all the work done by `MergeSort` across all its recursive calls.

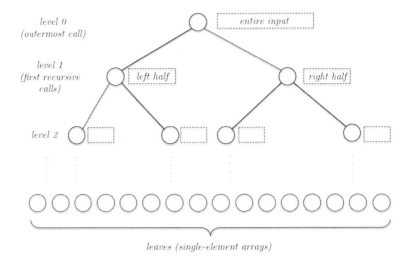

Figure 1.5: A recursion tree for `MergeSort`. Nodes correspond to recursive
calls. Level 0 corresponds to the outermost call to `MergeSort`, level 1 to its
recursive calls, and so on.

The root of the recursion tree corresponds to the outermost call
to `MergeSort`, where the input is the original input array. We'll call
this level 0 of the tree. Since each invocation of `MergeSort` spawns
two recursive calls, the tree will be binary (that is, with two children
per node). Level 1 of the tree has two nodes, corresponding to the
two recursive calls made by the outermost call, one for the left half
of the input array and one for the right half. Each of the level-1
recursive calls will itself make two recursive calls, each operating on a
particular quarter of the original input array. This process continues
until eventually the recursion bottoms out with arrays of size 0 or 1
(the base cases).

Quiz 1.1

Roughly how many levels does this recursion tree have, as a
function of the length n of the input array?

---

a) A constant number (independent of n)

b) $\log_2 n$

c) $\sqrt{n}$

d) n

(See Section 1.5.4 for the solution and discussion.)

This recursion tree suggests a particularly convenient way to account for the work done by MergeSort, which is level by level. To implement this idea, we need to understand two things: the number of distinct subproblems at a given recursion level j, and the length of the input to each of these subproblems.

Quiz 1.2

What is the pattern? Fill in the blanks in the following statement: at each level $j = 0, 1, 2, \ldots$ of the recursion tree, there are [blank] subproblems, each operating on a subarray of length [blank].

a) 2^j and 2^j, respectively

b) $n/2^j$ and $n/2^j$, respectively

c) 2^j and $n/2^j$, respectively

d) $n/2^j$ and 2^j, respectively

(See Section 1.5.4 for the solution and discussion.)

Let's now put this pattern to use and tally all the operations that MergeSort performs. We proceed level by level, so fix a level j of the recursion tree. How much work is done by the level-j recursive calls, not counting the work done by their recursive calls at later levels? Inspecting the MergeSort code, we see that it does only three things: make two recursive calls and invoke the Merge subroutine on the results. Thus ignoring the work done by later recursive calls, the work done by a level-j subproblem is just the work done by Merge.

This we already understand from Lemma 1.1: at most 6ℓ operations, where ℓ is the length of the input array to this subproblem.

To put everything together, we can express the total work done by level-j recursive calls (not counting later recursive calls) as

$$\underbrace{\text{\# of level-}j\text{ subproblems}}_{=2^j} \times \underbrace{\text{work per level-}j\text{ subproblem}}_{=6n/2^j}.$$

Using the solution to Quiz 1.2, we know that the first term equals 2^j, and the input length to each such subproblem is $n/2^j$. Taking $\ell = n/2^j$, Lemma 1.1 implies that each level-j subproblem performs at most $6n/2^j$ operations. We conclude that at most

$$2^j \cdot \frac{6n}{2^j} = 6n$$

operations are performed across all the recursive calls at the jth recursion level.

Remarkably, our bound on the work done at a given level j is independent of j! That is, each level of the recursion tree contributes the same number of operations to the analysis. The reason for this is a perfect equilibrium between two competing forces—the number of subproblems doubles every level, while the amount of work performed per subproblem halves every level.

We're interested in the number of operations performed across *all* levels of the recursion tree. By the solution to Quiz 1.1, the recursion tree has $\log_2 n + 1$ levels (levels 0 through $\log_2 n$, inclusive). Using our bound of $6n$ operations per level, we can bound the total number of operations by

$$\underbrace{\text{number of levels}}_{=\log_2 n+1} \times \underbrace{\text{work per level}}_{\leq 6n} \leq 6n\log_2 n + 6n,$$

matching the bound claimed in Theorem 1.2. $\mathcal{Q}\mathcal{E}\mathcal{D}$[17]

---

[17]"Q.e.d." is an abbreviation for *quod erat demonstrandum*, and means "that which was to be demonstrated." In mathematical writing, it is used at the end of a proof to mark its completion.

On Primitive Operations

We measure the running time of an algorithm like
MergeSort in terms of the number of "primitive operations" performed. Intuitively, a primitive operation
performs a simple task (like adding, comparing, or
copying) while touching a small number of simple
variables (like 32-bit integers).[18] Warning: in some
high-level programming languages, a single line of
code can mask a large number of primitive operations.
For example, a line of code that touches every element
of a long array translates to a number of primitive
operations proportional to the array's length.

1.5.4   Solutions to Quizzes 1.1–1.2

Solution to Quiz 1.1

Correct answer: (b). The correct answer is $\approx \log_2 n$. The reason
is that the input size decreases by a factor of two with each level of
the recursion. If the input length in level 0 is n, the level-1 recursive
calls operate on arrays of length $n/2$, the level-2 recursive calls on
arrays of length $n/4$, and so on. The recursion bottoms out at the
base cases, with input arrays of length at most one, where there are
no more recursive calls. How many levels of recursion are required?
The number of times you need to divide n by 2 before obtaining a
number that is at most 1. For n a power of 2, this is precisely the
definition of $\log_2 n$. (More generally, it is $\log_2 n$ rounded up to the
nearest integer.)

Solution to Quiz 1.2

Correct answer: (c). The correct answer is that there are 2^j distinct
subproblems at recursion level j, and each operates on a subarray
of length $n/2^j$. For the first point, start with level 0, where there is
one recursive call. There are two recursive calls as level 1, and more

---

[18]More precise definitions are possible, but we won't need them.

generally, since `MergeSort` calls itself twice, the number of recursive calls at each level is double the number at the previous level. This successive doubling implies that there are 2^j subproblems at each level j of the recursion tree. Similarly, since every recursive call gets only half the input of the previous one, after j levels of recursion the input length has dropped to $n/2^j$. Or for a different argument, we already know that there are 2^j subproblems at level j, and the original input array (of length n) is equally partitioned among these—exactly $n/2^j$ elements per subproblem.

1.6 Guiding Principles for the Analysis of Algorithms

With our first algorithm analysis under our belt (`MergeSort`, in Theorem 1.2), it's the right time to take a step back and make explicit three assumptions that informed our running time analysis and interpretation of it. We will adopt these three assumptions as guiding principles for how to reason about algorithms, and use them to define what we actually mean by a "fast algorithm."

The goal of these principles is to identify a sweet spot for the analysis of algorithms, one that balances accuracy with tractability. Exact running time analysis is possible only for the simplest algorithms; more generally, compromises are required. On the other hand, we don't want to throw out the baby with the bathwater—we still want our mathematical analysis to have predictive power about whether an algorithm will be fast or slow in practice. Once we find the right balance, we'll be able to prove good running time guarantees for dozens of fundamental algorithms, and these guarantees will paint an accurate picture of which algorithms tend to run faster than others.

1.6.1 Principle #1: Worst-Case Analysis

Our running time bound of $6n \log_2 n + 6n$ in Theorem 1.2 holds for *every* input array of length n, no matter what its contents. We made no assumptions about the input beyond its length n. Hypothetically, if there was an adversary whose sole purpose in life was to concoct a malevolent input designed to make `MergeSort` run as slow as possible, the $6n \log_2 n + 6n$ bound would still apply. This type of analysis is called *worst-case analysis*, since it gives a running time bound that is valid even for the "worst" inputs.

Given how naturally worst-case analysis fell out of our analysis of MergeSort, you might well wonder what else we could do. One alternative approach is "average-case analysis," which analyzes the average running time of an algorithm under some assumption about the relative frequencies of different inputs. For example, in the sorting problem, we could assume that all input arrays are equally likely and then study the average running time of different sorting algorithms. A second alternative is to look only at the performance of an algorithm on a small collection of "benchmark instances" that are thought to be representative of "typical" or "real-world" inputs.

Both average-case analysis and the analysis of benchmark instances can be useful when you have domain knowledge about your problem, and some understanding of which inputs are more representative than others. Worst-case analysis, in which you make absolutely no assumptions about the input, is particularly appropriate for general-purpose subroutines designed to work well across a range of application domains. To be useful to as many people as possible, these books focus on such general-purpose subroutines and, accordingly, use worst-case analysis to judge algorithm performance.

As a bonus, worst-case analysis is usually much more tractable mathematically than its alternatives. This is one reason why worst-case analysis naturally popped out of our MergeSort analysis, even though we had no a priori focus on worst-case inputs.

1.6.2   Principle #2: Big-Picture Analysis

The second and third guiding principles are closely related. Let's call the second one *big-picture analysis* (warning: this is not a standard term). This principle states that we should not worry unduly about small constant factors or lower-order terms in running time bounds. We've already seen this philosophy at work in our analysis of MergeSort: when analyzing the running time of the Merge subroutine (Lemma 1.1), we first proved an upper bound of $4\ell + 2$ on the number of operations (where ℓ is the length of the output array) and then settled for the simpler upper bound of 6ℓ, even though it suffers from a larger constant factor. How do we justify being so fast and loose with constant factors?

Mathematical tractability. The first reason for big-picture analysis is that it's way easier mathematically than the alternative of pinning down precise constant factors or lower-order terms. This point was already evident in our analysis of the running time of MergeSort.

Constants depend on environment-specific factors. The second justification is less obvious but extremely important. At the level of granularity we'll use to describe algorithms, as with the MergeSort algorithm, it would be totally misguided to obsess over exactly what the constant factors are. For example, during our analysis of the Merge subroutine, there was ambiguity about exactly how many "primitive operations" are performed each loop iteration (4, 5, or something else?). Thus different interpretations of the same pseudocode can lead to different constant factors. The ambiguity only increases once pseudocode gets translated into a concrete implementation in some high-level programming language, and then translated further into machine code—the constant factors will inevitably depend on the programming language used, the specific implementation, and the details of the compiler and processor. Our goal is to focus on properties of algorithms that transcend the details of the programming language and machine architecture, and these properties should be independent of small constant-factor changes in a running time bound.

Lose little predictive power. The third justification is simply that we're going to be able to get away with it. You might be concerned that ignoring constant factors would lead us astray, tricking us into thinking that an algorithm is fast when it is actually slow in practice, or vice versa. Happily, this won't happen for the algorithms discussed in these books.[19] Even though we won't be keeping track of lower-order terms and constant factors, the qualitative predictions of our mathematical analysis will be highly accurate—when analysis suggests that an algorithm should be fast, it will in fact be fast in practice, and conversely. So while big-picture analysis does discard some information, it preserves what we really care about: accurate guidance about which algorithms tend to be faster than others.[20]

---

[19]With one possible exception, the deterministic linear-time selection algorithm in the optional Section 6.3.

[20]It's still useful to have a general sense of the relevant constant factors, however. For example, in the highly tuned versions of MergeSort that you'll

1.6.3   Principle #3: Asymptotic Analysis

Our third and final guiding principle is to use *asymptotic analysis* and focus on the rate of growth of an algorithm's running time, as the input size n grows large. This bias toward large inputs was already evident when we interpreted our running time bound for MergeSort (Theorem 1.2), of $6n \log_2 n + 6n$ operations. We then cavalierly declared that MergeSort is "better than" simpler sorting methods with running time quadratic in the input size, such as InsertionSort. But is this really true?

For concreteness, suppose we have a sorting algorithm that performs at most $\frac{1}{2}n^2$ operations when sorting an array of length n, and consider the comparison

$$6n \log_2 n + 6n \quad \text{vs.} \quad \frac{1}{2}n^2.$$

Looking at the behavior of these two functions in Figure 1.6(a), we see that $\frac{1}{2}n^2$ is the smaller expression when n is small (at most 90 or so), while $6n \log_2 n + 6n$ is smaller for all larger n. So when we say that MergeSort is faster than simpler sorting methods, what we really mean is that it is faster on *sufficiently large instances*.

Why should we care more about large instances than small ones? Because large problems are the only ones that require algorithmic ingenuity. Almost any sorting method you can think of would sort an array of length 1000 instantaneously on a modern computer—there's no need to learn about divide-and-conquer algorithms.

Given that computers are constantly getting faster, you might wonder if all computational problems will eventually become trivial to solve. In fact, the faster computers get, the more relevant asymptotic analysis becomes. Our computational ambitions have always grown with our computational power, so as time goes on, we will consider larger and larger problem sizes. And the gulf in performance between algorithms with different asymptotic running times only becomes wider as inputs grow larger. For example, Figure 1.6(b) shows the difference between the functions $6n \log_2 n + 6n$ and $\frac{1}{2}n^2$ for larger (but still modest) values of n, and by the time $n = 1500$ there is roughly a

---

find in many programming libraries, the algorithm switches from MergeSort over to InsertionSort (for its better constant factor) once the input array length becomes small (for example, at most seven elements).

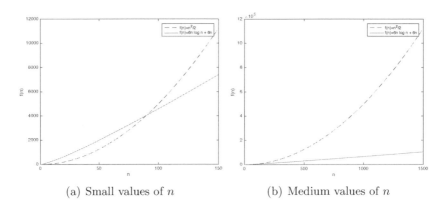

(a) Small values of n (b) Medium values of n

Figure 1.6: The function $\frac{1}{2}n^2$ grows much more quickly than $6n \log_2 n + 6n$ as n grows large. The scales of the x- and y-axes in (b) are one and two orders of magnitude, respectively, bigger than those in (a).

factor-10 difference between them. If we scaled n up by another factor of 10, or 100, or 1000 to start reaching interesting problem sizes, the difference between the two functions would be huge.

For a different way to think about asymptotic analysis, suppose you have a fixed time budget, like an hour or a day. How does the solvable problem size scale with additional computing power? With an algorithm that runs in time proportional to the input size, a four-fold increase in computing power lets you solve problems four times as large as before. With an algorithm that runs in time proportional to the square of the input size, you would be able to solve problems that are only twice as large as before.

1.6.4 What Is a "Fast" Algorithm?

Our three guiding principles lead us to the following definition of a "fast algorithm:"

> A "fast algorithm" is an algorithm whose worst-case running time grows slowly with the input size.

Our first guiding principle, that we want running time guarantees that do not assume any domain knowledge, is the reason why we focus on the worst-case running time of an algorithm. Our second and third guiding principles, that constant factors are language- and machine-dependent and that large problems are the interesting ones, are the reasons why we focus on the rate of growth of the running time of an algorithm.

What do we mean that the running time of an algorithm "grows slowly?" For almost all of the problems we'll discuss, the holy grail is a *linear-time algorithm*, meaning an algorithm with running time proportional to the input size. Linear time is even better than our bound on the running time of `MergeSort`, which is proportional to $n \log n$ and hence modestly super-linear. We will succeed in designing linear-time algorithms for some problems but not for others. In any case, it is the best-case scenario to which we will aspire.

For-Free Primitives

We can think of an algorithm with linear or near-linear running time as a primitive that we can use essentially "for free," because the amount of computation used is barely more than the amount required just to read the input. Sorting is a canonical example of a for-free primitive, and we will also learn several others. When you have a primitive relevant for your problem that is so blazingly fast, why not use it? For example, you can always sort your data in a preprocessing step, even if you're not quite sure how it will help later. One of the goals of this book series is to stock your algorithmic toolbox with as many for-free primitives as possible, ready to be applied at will.

The Upshot

☆ An algorithm is a set of well-defined rules for solving some computational problem.

☆ The number of primitive operations performed by the algorithm you learned in grade school to multiply two n-digit integers scales as a quadratic function of the number n.

☆ Karatsuba multiplication is a recursive algorithm for integer multiplication, and it uses Gauss's trick to save one recursive call over a more straightforward recursive algorithm.

☆ Seasoned programmers and computer scientists generally think and communicate about algorithms using high-level descriptions rather than detailed implementations.

☆ The `MergeSort` algorithm is a "divide-and-conquer" algorithm that splits the input array into two halves, recursively sorts each half, and combines the results using the `Merge` subroutine.

☆ Ignoring constant factors and lower-order terms, the number of operations performed by `MergeSort` to sort n elements grows like the function $n \log_2 n$. The analysis uses a recursion tree to conveniently organize the work done by all the recursive calls.

☆ Because the function $\log_2 n$ grows slowly with n, `MergeSort` is typically faster than simpler sorting algorithms, which all require a quadratic number of operations. For large n, the improvement is dramatic.

☆ Three guiding principles for the analysis of algorithms are: (i) worst-case analysis, to promote general-purpose algorithms that work well with no assumptions about the input; (ii) big-picture analysis, which balances predictive power with mathematical tractability by ignoring constant factors and lower-order terms; and (iii) asymptotic analysis, which is a bias toward large inputs, which are the inputs that require algorithmic ingenuity.

☆ A "fast algorithm" is an algorithm whose worst-case running time grows slowly with the input size.

☆ A "for-free primitive" is an algorithm that runs in linear or near-linear time, barely more than what is required to read the input.

Test Your Understanding

Problem 1.1 *(S)* Suppose we run MergeSort on the following input array:

5	3	8	9	1	7	0	2	6	4

Fast forward to the moment after the two outermost recursive calls complete, but before the final Merge step. Thinking of the two 5-element output arrays of the recursive calls as a glued-together 10-element array, which number is in the 7th position?

Problem 1.2 Consider the following modification to the MergeSort algorithm: divide the input array into thirds (rather than halves), recursively sort each third, and finally combine the results using a three-way Merge subroutine. What is the running time of this algorithm as a function of the length n of the input array, ignoring constant factors and lower-order terms? [Hint: Note that the Merge subroutine can still be implemented so that the number of operations is only linear in the sum of the input array lengths.]

a) n

b) $n \log n$

c) $n(\log n)^2$

d) $n^2 \log n$

Problem 1.3 Suppose you are given k sorted arrays, each with n elements, and you want to combine them into a single array of kn

elements. One approach is to use the `Merge` subroutine from Section 1.4.5 repeatedly, first merging the first two arrays, then merging the result with the third array, then with the fourth array, and so on until you merge in the kth and final input array. What is the running time taken by this successive merging algorithm, as a function of k and n, ignoring constant factors and lower-order terms?

a) $n \log k$

b) nk

c) $nk \log k$

d) $nk \log n$

e) nk^2

f) $n^2 k$

Problem 1.4 *(S)* Consider again the problem of merging k sorted length-n arrays into a single sorted length-kn array. Consider the algorithm that first divides the k arrays into $k/2$ pairs of arrays, and uses the `Merge` subroutine to combine each pair, resulting in $k/2$ sorted length-$2n$ arrays. The algorithm repeats this step until there is only one length-kn sorted array. What is the running time of this procedure, as a function of k and n, ignoring constant factors and lower-order terms?

a) $n \log k$

b) nk

c) $nk \log k$

d) $nk \log n$

e) nk^2

f) $n^2 k$

Challenge Problems

Problem 1.5 You are given as input an unsorted array of n distinct numbers, where n is a power of 2. Give an algorithm that identifies the second-largest number in the array, and that uses at most $n + \log_2 n - 2$ comparisons.

[Hint: Consider computing the largest number using a knockout tournament. What information do you have left over?]

Programming Problems

Problem 1.6 Implement Karatsuba's integer multiplication algorithm in your favorite programming language.[21] To get the most out of this problem, your program should invoke the language's multiplication operator only on pairs of single-digit numbers.

For a concrete challenge, what's the product of the following two 64-digit numbers?[22]

3141592653589793238462643383279502884197169399375105820974944592

2718281828459045235360287471352662497757247093699959574966967627

---

[21]Food for thought: does it make your life easier if the number of digits of each integer is a power of 2?

[22]If you need help or want to compare notes with other readers, visit the discussion forums at www.algorithmsilluminated.org.

Chapter 2

Asymptotic Notation

This chapter develops the mathematical formalism that encodes our guiding principles for the analysis of algorithms (Section 1.6). The goal is to identify a sweet spot of granularity for reasoning about algorithms—we want to suppress second-order details like constant factors and lower-order terms, and focus on how the running time of an algorithm scales as the input size grows. This is done formally through big-O notation and its relatives—concepts that belong in the vocabulary of every serious programmer and computer scientist.

2.1 The Gist

Before getting into the mathematical formalism of asymptotic notation, let's make sure the topic is well motivated, that you have a strong sense of what it's trying to accomplish, and that you've seen a couple of simple and intuitive examples.

2.1.1 Motivation

Asymptotic notation provides the basic vocabulary for discussing the design and analysis of algorithms. It's important that you know what programmers mean when they say that one piece of code runs in "big-O of n time," while another runs in "big-O of n-squared time."

This vocabulary is so ubiquitous because it identifies the right "sweet spot" for reasoning about algorithms. Asymptotic notation is coarse enough to suppress all the details you want to ignore—details that depend on the choice of architecture, the choice of programming language, the choice of compiler, and so on. On the other hand, it's precise enough to make useful comparisons between different high-level algorithmic approaches to solving a problem, especially on larger inputs (the inputs that require algorithmic ingenuity). For example, asymptotic analysis helps us differentiate between better and worse approaches to sorting, better and worse approaches to multiplying two integers, and so on.

2.1.2   The High-Level Idea

If you ask a practicing programmer to explain the point of asymptotic notation, he or she is likely to say something like the following:

Asymptotic Notation in Seven Words

suppress $\underbrace{\textit{constant factors}}_{\textit{too system-dependent}}$ *and* $\underbrace{\textit{lower-order terms}}_{\textit{irrelevant for large inputs}}$

We'll see that there's more to asymptotic notation than just these seven words, but ten years from now, if you remember only seven words about it, these are good ones.

When analyzing the running time of an algorithm, why would we want to throw away information like constant factors and lower-order terms? Lower-order terms, by definition, become increasingly irrelevant as you focus on large inputs, which are the inputs that require algorithmic ingenuity. Meanwhile, the constant factors are generally highly dependent on the details of the environment. If we don't want to commit to a specific programming language, architecture, or compiler when analyzing an algorithm, it makes sense to use a formalism that does not focus on constant factors.

For example, remember when we analyzed MergeSort (Section 1.4)? We gave an upper bound on its running time of

$$6n \log_2 n + 6n$$

primitive operations, where n is the length of the input array. The lower-order term here is the $6n$, as n grows more slowly than $n \log_2 n$, so it will be suppressed in asymptotic notation. The leading constant factor of 6 also gets suppressed, leaving us with the much simpler expression of $n \log n$. We would then say that the running time of MergeSort is "big-O of $n \log n$," written $O(n \log n)$, or that MergeSort is an "$O(n \log n)$-time algorithm."[1]   Intuitively, saying that something is $O(f(n))$ for a function $f(n)$ means that $f(n)$ is what you're left with after suppressing constant factors and lower-order terms.[2] This "big-O notation" buckets algorithms into groups according to their asymptotic worst-case running times—the linear $(O(n))$-time algorithms, the $O(n \log n)$-time algorithms, the quadratic $(O(n^2))$-time algorithms, the constant $(O(1))$-time algorithms, and so on.

To be clear, I'm certainly not claiming that constant factors never matter in algorithm design. Rather, when you want to make a comparison between fundamentally different ways of solving a problem, asymptotic analysis is often the right tool for understanding which one is going to perform better, especially on reasonably large inputs. Once you've figured out the best high-level algorithmic approach to a problem, you might well want to work harder to improve the leading constant factor, and perhaps even the lower-order terms. By all means, if the future of your start-up depends on how efficiently you implement a particular piece of code, have at it and make it as fast as you can.

2.1.3   Four Examples

We conclude this section with four very simple examples. They are so simple that, if you have any prior experience with big-O notation, you should probably just skip straight to Section 2.2 to start learning the mathematical formalism. But if these concepts are completely new to you, these simple examples should get you properly oriented.

Consider first the problem of searching an array for a given integer t. Let's analyze the straightforward algorithm that performs a linear scan through the array, checking each entry to see if it is the desired integer t.

---

[1]When ignoring constant factors, we don't even need to specify the base of the logarithm (as different logarithmic functions differ only by a constant factor). See Section 4.2.2 for further discussion.

[2]For example, even the function $10^{100} \cdot n$ is technically $O(n)$. In these books, we will only study running time bounds where the suppressed constant factor is reasonably small.

Searching One Array

Input: array A of n integers, and an integer t.
Output: Whether or not A contains t.

---

for $i := 1$ to n **do**
    if $A[i] = t$ **then**
        return TRUE
return FALSE

This code just checks each array entry in turn. If it ever finds the integer t it returns true, and if it falls off the end of the array without finding t it returns false.

We haven't formally defined what big-O notation means yet, but from our intuitive discussion so far you might be able to guess the asymptotic running time of the code above.

Quiz 2.1

What is the asymptotic running time of the code above for searching one array, as a function of the array length n?

    a) $O(1)$

    b) $O(\log n)$

    c) $O(n)$

    d) $O(n^2)$

(See Section 2.1.4 for the solution and discussion.)

Our final three examples concern different ways of combining two loops. First, let's think about one loop followed by another. Suppose we're now given two integer arrays A and B, both of length n, and we want to know whether a target integer t is in either one. Let's again consider the straightforward algorithm, where we just search through A, and if we fail to find t in A, we then search through B. If we don't find t in B either, we return false.

Searching Two Arrays

Input: arrays A and B of n integers each, and an integer t.

Output: Whether or not A or B contains t.

---

for $i := 1$ to n **do**
    if $A[i] = t$ **then**
        return TRUE
for $i := 1$ to n **do**
    if $B[i] = t$ **then**
        return TRUE
return FALSE

What, in big-O notation, is the running time of this longer piece of code?

Quiz 2.2

What is the asymptotic running time of the code above for searching two arrays, as a function of the array lengths n?

a) $O(1)$

b) $O(\log n)$

c) $O(n)$

d) $O(n^2)$

(See Section 2.1.4 for the solution and discussion.)

Next let's look at a more interesting example of two loops that are nested, rather than in sequence. Suppose we want to check whether or not two given arrays of length n have a number in common. The simplest solution is to check all possibilities. That is, for each index i into the array A and each index j into the array B, we check if $A[i]$ is the same number as $B[j]$. If it is, we return true. If we exhaust all the possibilities without ever finding equal elements, we can safely return false.

Checking for a Common Element

Input: arrays A and B of n integers each.
Output: Whether or not there is an integer t
contained in both A and B.

```
for i := 1 to n do
    for j := 1 to n do
        if A[i] = B[j] then
            return TRUE
return FALSE
```

The question is the usual one: in big-O notation, what is the running
time of this piece of code?

Quiz 2.3

What is the asymptotic running time of the code above for
checking for a common element, as a function of the array
lengths n?

   a) $O(1)$

   b) $O(\log n)$

   c) $O(n)$

   d) $O(n^2)$

(See Section 2.1.4 for the solution and discussion.)

Our final example again involves nested loops, but this time
we're looking for duplicate entries in a single array A, rather than
in two different arrays. Here's the piece of code we're going to
analyze.

Checking for Duplicates

Input: array A of n integers.
Output: Whether or not A contains an integer more than once.

---

for $i := 1$ to n **do**
    for $j := i + 1$ to n **do**
        if $A[i] = A[j]$ **then**
            return TRUE
  return FALSE

There are two small differences between this piece of code and the previous one. The first and more obvious change is that we're comparing the ith element of A to the jth element of A, rather than to the jth element of some other array B. The second and more subtle change is that the inner loop now begins at the index $i + 1$ rather than the index 1. Why not start at 1, like before? Because then it would also return true in the very first iteration (since clearly $A[1] = A[1]$), whether or not the array has any duplicate entries! Correctness could be salvaged by skipping all the iterations where i and j are equal, but this would still be wasteful: each pair of elements $A[h]$ and $A[k]$ of A would be compared to each other twice (once when $i = h$ and $j = k$ and once when $i = k$ and $j = h$), while the code above compares them only once.

The question is the usual one: in big-O notation, what is the running time of this piece of code?

Quiz 2.4

What is the asymptotic running time of the code above for checking for duplicates, as a function of the array length n?

a) $O(1)$

b) $O(\log n)$

c) $O(n)$

d) $O(n^2)$

(See Section 2.1.4 for the solution and discussion.)

These basic examples should have given you a strong intuitive sense of how big-O notation is defined and what it is trying to accomplish. Next we move on to both the mathematical development of asymptotic notation and some more interesting algorithms.

2.1.4   Solutions to Quizzes 2.1–2.4

Solution to Quiz 2.1

Correct answer: (c). The correct answer is $O(n)$. Equivalently, we say that the algorithm has running time *linear in n*. Why is that true? The exact number of operations performed depends on the input—whether or not the target t is contained in the array A and, if so, where in the array it lies. In the worst case, when t is not in the array, the code will do an unsuccessful search, scanning through the entire array (over n loop iterations) and returning false. The key observation is that the code performs a constant number of operations for each entry of the array (comparing $A[i]$ with t, incrementing the loop index i, etc.). Here "constant" means some number independent of n, like 2 or 3. We could argue about exactly what this constant is in the code above, but whatever it is, it is conveniently suppressed in the big-O notation. Similarly, the code does a constant number of operations before the loop begins and after it ends, and whatever the exact constant may be, it constitutes a lower-order term that is suppressed in the big-O notation. Since ignoring constant factors and lower-order terms leaves us with a bound of n on the total number of operations, the asymptotic running time of this code is $O(n)$.

Solution to Quiz 2.2

Correct answer: (c). The answer is the same as before, $O(n)$. The reason is that the worst-case number of operations performed (in an unsuccessful search) is twice that of the previous piece of code—first we search the first array, and then the second array. This extra factor of 2 contributes only to the leading constant in the running time bound and is therefore suppressed when we use big-O notation. So this algorithm, like the previous one, is a linear-time algorithm.

Solution to Quiz 2.3

Correct answer: (d). This time, the answer has changed. For this piece of code, the running time is not $O(n)$, but is $O(n^2)$. ("Big-O of n squared," also called a "quadratic-time algorithm.") So with this algorithm, if you multiply the lengths of the input arrays by 10, the running time will go up by a factor of 100 (rather than a factor of 10 for a linear-time algorithm).

Why does this code have a running time of $O(n^2)$? The code again does a constant number of operations for each loop iteration (that is, for each choice of the indices i and j) and a constant number of operations outside the loops. What's different is that there's now a total of n^2 iterations of this double for loop—one for each choice of $i \in \{1, 2, \ldots, n\}$ and $j \in \{1, 2, \ldots, n\}$. In our first example, there were only n iterations of a single for loop. In our second example, because the first for loop completed before the second one began, we had only $2n$ iterations overall. Here, for *each* of the n iterations of the outer for loop, the code performs n iterations of the inner for loop. This gives $n \times n = n^2$ iterations in all.

Solution to Quiz 2.4

Correct answer: (d). The answer to this question is the same as the last one, $O(n^2)$. The running time is again proportional to the number of iterations of the double for loop (with a constant number of operations per iteration). So how many iterations are there? The answer is roughly $\frac{n^2}{2}$. One way to see this is to remember that this piece of code does roughly half the work of the previous one (since the inner for loop starts at $j = i + 1$ rather than $j = 1$). A second way is to observe that there is exactly one iteration for each subset $\{i, j\}$ of two distinct indices from $\{1, 2, \ldots, n\}$, and there are precisely $\binom{n}{2} = \frac{n(n-1)}{2}$ such subsets.[3]

---

[3] $\binom{n}{2}$ is pronounced "n choose 2," and is also sometimes referred to as a "binomial coefficient." See also the solution to Quiz 3.1.

2.2   Big-O Notation

This section presents the formal definition of big-O notation. We begin with a definition in plain English, illustrate it pictorially, and finally give the mathematical definition.

2.2.1   English Definition

Big-O notation concerns functions $T(n)$ defined on the positive integers $n = 1, 2, \ldots$. For us, $T(n)$ will almost always denote a bound on the worst-case running time of an algorithm, as a function of the size n of the input. What does it mean to say that $T(n) = O(f(n))$, for some "canonical" function $f(n)$, like n, $n \log n$, or n^2? Here's the definition in English.

Big-O Notation (English Version)

$T(n) = O(f(n))$ if and only if $T(n)$ is eventually bounded above by a constant multiple of $f(n)$.

2.2.2   Pictorial Definition

See Figure 2.1 for a pictorial illustration of the definition of big-O notation. The x-axis corresponds to the parameter n, the y-axis to the value of a function. Let $T(n)$ be the function corresponding to the solid line, and $f(n)$ the lower dashed line. $T(n)$ is not bounded above by $f(n)$, but multiplying $f(n)$ by 3 results in the upper dashed line, which does lie above $T(n)$ once we go far enough to the right on the graph, after the "crossover point" at n_0. Since $T(n)$ is indeed eventually bounded above by a constant multiple of $f(n)$, we can say that $T(n) = O(f(n))$.

2.2.3   Mathematical Definition

Here is the mathematical definition of big-O notation, the definition you should use in formal proofs.

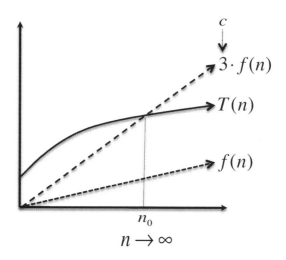

Figure 2.1: A picture illustrating when $T(n) = O(f(n))$. The constant c quantifies the "constant multiple" of $f(n)$, and the constant n_0 quantifies "eventually."

Big-O Notation (Mathematical Version)

$T(n) = O(f(n))$ if and only if there exist positive constants c and n_0 such that

$$T(n) \leq c \cdot f(n) \qquad (2.1)$$

for all $n \geq n_0$.

This is a direct translation of the English definition in Section 2.2.1. The inequality in (2.1) expresses that $T(n)$ should be bounded above by a multiple of $f(n)$ (with the constant c specifying the multiple). The "for all $n \geq n_0$" expresses that the inequality only needs to hold eventually, once n is sufficiently large (with the constant n_0 specifying how large). For example, in Figure 2.1, the constant c corresponds to 3, while n_0 corresponds to the crossover point between the functions $T(n)$ and $c \cdot f(n)$.

A game-theoretic view. If you want to prove that $T(n) = O(f(n))$, for example to prove that the asymptotic running time of an algorithm is linear in the input size (corresponding to $f(n) = n$), then your task is to choose the constants c and n_0 so that (2.1) holds whenever $n \geq n_0$. One way to think about this is game-theoretically, as a contest between you and an opponent. You go first, and have to commit to constants c and n_0. Your opponent goes second and can choose any integer n that is at least n_0. You win if (2.1) holds, your opponent wins if the opposite inequality $T(n) > c \cdot f(n)$ holds.

If $T(n) = O(f(n))$, then there are constants c and n_0 such that (2.1) holds for all $n \geq n_0$, and you have a winning strategy in this game. Otherwise, no matter how you choose c and n_0, your opponent can choose a large enough $n \geq n_0$ to flip the inequality and win the game.

A Word of Caution

When we say that c and n_0 are constants, we mean they *cannot depend on* n. For example, in Figure 2.1, c and n_0 were fixed numbers (like 3 or 1000), and we then considered the inequality (2.1) as n grows arbitrarily large (looking rightward on the graph toward infinity). If you ever find yourself saying "take $n_0 = n$" or "take $c = \log_2 n$" in an alleged big-O proof, you need to start over with choices of c and n_0 that are independent of n.

2.3   Two Basic Examples

Having slogged through the formal definition of big-O notation, let's look at a couple of examples. These examples won't provide us with any insights we don't already have, but they serve as an important sanity check that big-O notation is achieving its intended goal, of suppressing constant factors and lower-order terms. They are also a good warm-up for the less obvious examples we will encounter later.

2.3.1   Degree-k Polynomials are $O(n^k)$

Our first formal claim is that if $T(n)$ is a polynomial with some degree k, then $T(n) = O(n^k)$.

Proposition 2.1 *Suppose*

$$T(n) = a_k n^k + \cdots a_1 n + a_0,$$

where $k \geq 0$ is a nonnegative integer and the a_i's are real numbers (positive or negative). Then $T(n) = O(n^k)$.

Proposition 2.1 says that with a polynomial, in big-O notation, all you need to worry about is the highest degree that appears in the polynomial. Thus, big-O notation really is suppressing constant factors and lower-order terms.

Proof of Proposition 2.1: To prove this proposition, we need to use the mathematical definition of big-O notation (Section 2.2.3). To satisfy the definition, it's our job to find a pair of positive constants c and n_0 (each independent of n), with c quantifying the constant multiple of n^k and n_0 quantifying "sufficiently large n." To keep things easy to follow but admittedly mysterious, let's pull values for these constants out of a hat: $n_0 = 1$ and c equal to the sum of absolute values of the coefficients:[4]

$$c = |a_k| + \cdots + |a_1| + |a_0|.$$

Both of these numbers are independent of n. We now need to show that these choices of constants satisfy the definition, meaning that $T(n) \leq c \cdot n^k$ for all $n \geq n_0 = 1$.

To verify this inequality, fix an arbitrary positive integer $n \geq n_0 = 1$. We need a sequence of upper bounds on $T(n)$, culminating in an upper bound of $c \cdot n^k$. First let's apply the definition of $T(n)$:

$$T(n) = a_k n^k + \cdots + a_1 n + a_0.$$

If we take the absolute value of each coefficient a_i on the right-hand side, the expression only becomes larger. ($|a_i|$ can only be bigger than a_i, and since n^i is positive, $|a_i|n^i$ can only be bigger than $a_i n^i$.) This means that

$$T(n) \leq |a_k| n^k + \cdots + |a_1| n + |a_0|.$$

Why is this step useful? Now that the coefficients are nonnegative, we can use a similar trick to turn the different powers of n into a

---

[4]Recall that the *absolute value* $|x|$ of a real number x equals x when $x \geq 0$, and $-x$ when $x \leq 0$. In particular, $|x|$ is always nonnegative.

common power of n. Since $n \geq 1$, n^k is only bigger than n^i for every $i \in \{0, 1, 2, \ldots, k\}$. Since $|a_i|$ is nonnegative, $|a_i|n^k$ is only bigger than $|a_i|n^i$. This means that

$$T(n) \leq |a_k|n^k + \cdots + |a_1|n^k + |a_0|n^k = \underbrace{(|a_k| + \cdots + |a_1| + |a_0|)}_{=c} \cdot n^k.$$

This inequality holds for every $n \geq n_0 = 1$, which is exactly what we wanted to prove. $\mathcal{QED}$

How do you know how to choose the constants c and n_0? The usual approach is to reverse engineer them. This involves going through a derivation like the one above and figuring out on-the-fly the choices of constants that let you push the proof through. We'll see some examples of this method in Section 2.5.

2.3.2   Degree-k Polynomials Are Not $O(n^{k-1})$

Our second example is really a non-example: a degree-k polynomial is $O(n^k)$, but is not generally $O(n^{k-1})$.

Proposition 2.2 *Let $k \geq 1$ be a positive integer and define $T(n) = n^k$. Then $T(n)$ is not $O(n^{k-1})$.*

Proposition 2.2 implies that polynomials with distinct degrees are distinct with respect to big-O notation. (If this weren't true, something would be wrong with our definition of big-O notation!)

Proof of Proposition 2.2: The best way to prove that one function is not big-O of another is usually with a proof by contradiction. In this type of proof, you assume the *opposite* of what you want to prove, and then build on this assumption with a sequence of logically correct steps that culminates in a patently false statement. Such a contradiction implies that the assumption can't be true, and this proves the desired statement.

So, assume that n^k is in fact $O(n^{k-1})$; we proceed to derive a contradiction. What does it mean if $n^k = O(n^{k-1})$? That n^k is eventually bounded by a constant multiple of n^{k-1}. That is, there are positive constants c and n_0 such that

$$n^k \leq c \cdot n^{k-1}$$

for all $n \geq n_0$. Since n is a positive number, we can cancel n^{k-1} from both sides of this inequality to derive

$$n \leq c$$

for all $n \geq n_0$. This inequality asserts that the constant c is bigger than every positive integer, a patently false statement (for a counterexample, take $c + 1$, rounded up to the nearest integer). This shows that our original assumption that $n^k = O(n^{k-1})$ cannot be correct, and we can conclude that n^k is not $O(n^{k-1})$. $\mathcal{QED}$

2.4   Big-Omega and Big-Theta Notation

Big-O notation is by far the most important and ubiquitous concept for discussing the asymptotic running time of algorithms. A couple of its close relatives, the big-omega and big-theta notations, are also worth knowing. If big-O is analogous to "less than or equal to ($\leq$)," then big-omega and big-theta are analogous to "greater than or equal to ($\geq$)," and "equal to ($=$)," respectively. Let's now treat them a little more precisely.

2.4.1   Big-Omega Notation

The formal definition of big-omega notation parallels that of big-O notation. In English, we say that one function $T(n)$ is big-omega of another function $f(n)$ if and only if $T(n)$ is eventually bounded below by a constant multiple of $f(n)$. In this case, we write $T(n) = \Omega(f(n))$. As before, we use two constants c and n_0 to quantify "constant multiple" and "eventually."

Big-Omega Notation (Mathematical Version)

$T(n) = \Omega(f(n))$ if and only if there exist positive constants c and n_0 such that

$$T(n) \geq c \cdot f(n)$$

for all $n \geq n_0$.

You can imagine what the corresponding picture looks like:

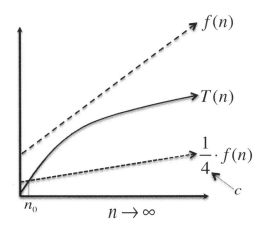

$T(n)$ again corresponds to the function with the solid line. The function $f(n)$ is the upper dashed line. This function does not bound $T(n)$ from below, but if we multiply it by the constant $c = \frac{1}{4}$, the result (the lower dashed line) does bound $T(n)$ from below for all n past the crossover point at n_0. Thus $T(n) = \Omega(f(n))$.

2.4.2   Big-Theta Notation

Big-theta notation, or simply theta notation, is analogous to "equal to." Saying that $T(n) = \Theta(f(n))$ just means that both $T(n) = \Omega(f(n))$ and $T(n) = O(f(n))$. Equivalently, $T(n)$ is eventually sandwiched between two different constant multiples of $f(n)$.[5]

Big-Theta Notation (Mathematical Version)

$T(n) = \Theta(f(n))$ if and only if there exist positive constants c_1, c_2, and n_0 such that

$$c_1 \cdot f(n) \leq T(n) \leq c_2 \cdot f(n)$$

for all $n \geq n_0$.

---

[5] Proving this equivalence amounts to showing that one version of the definition is satisfied if and only if the other one is. If $T(n) = \Theta(f(n))$ according to the second definition, then the constants c_2 and n_0 prove that $T(n) = O(f(n))$, while the constants c_1 and n_0 prove that $T(n) = \Omega(f(n))$. In the other direction, suppose you can prove that $T(n) = O(f(n))$ using the constants c_2 and n_0' and $T(n) = \Omega(f(n))$ using the constants c_1 and n_0''. Then $T(n) = \Theta(f(n))$ in the sense of the second definition, with constants c_1, c_2, and $n_0 = \max\{n_0', n_0''\}$.

A Word of Caution

Algorithm designers often use big-O notation even when big-theta notation would be more accurate. This book will follow that tradition. For example, consider a subroutine that scans an array of length n, performing a constant number of operations per entry (like the `Merge` subroutine in Section 1.4.5). The running time of such a subroutine is obviously $\Theta(n)$, but it's common to only mention that it is $O(n)$. This is because, as algorithm designers, we generally focus on upper bounds—guarantees about how long our algorithms could possibly run.

The next quiz checks your understanding of big-O, big-omega, and big-theta notation.

Quiz 2.5

Let $T(n) = \frac{1}{2}n^2 + 3n$. Which of the following statements are true? (There might be more than one correct answer.)

a) $T(n) = O(n)$

b) $T(n) = \Omega(n)$

c) $T(n) = \Theta(n^2)$

d) $T(n) = O(n^3)$

(See Section 2.4.5 for the solution and discussion.)

2.4.3   Little-O Notation

There's one final piece of asymptotic notation, "little-o notation," that you see from time to time. If big-O notation is analogous to "less than or equal to," little-o notation is analogous to "strictly less than."[6]

---

[6]Similarly, there is a "little-omega" notation that corresponds to "strictly greater than," but we won't have occasion to use it. There is no "little-theta"

Little-O Notation (Mathematical Version)

$T(n) = o(f(n))$ if and only if for every positive constant $c > 0$, there exists a choice of n_0 such that

$$T(n) \leq c \cdot f(n) \qquad (2.2)$$

for all $n \geq n_0$.

Proving that one function is big-O of another requires only two constants c and n_0, chosen once and for all. To prove that one function is little-o of another, we have to prove something stronger, that for *every* constant c, no matter how small, $T(n)$ is eventually bounded above by the constant multiple $c \cdot f(n)$. Note that the constant n_0 chosen to quantify "eventually" can depend on c (but not n!), with smaller constants c generally requiring bigger constants n_0. For example, for every positive integer k, $n^{k-1} = o(n^k)$.[7]

2.4.4   Where Does Notation Come From?

Asymptotic notation was not invented by computer scientists—it has been used in number theory since around the turn of the 20th century. Donald E. Knuth, the grandfather of the formal analysis of algorithms, proposed using it as the standard language for discussing rates of growth, and in particular for algorithm running times.

> "On the basis of the issues discussed here, I propose that members of SIGACT,[8] and editors of computer science and mathematics journals, adopt the O, Ω, and Θ notations as defined above, unless a better alternative can be found reasonably soon."[9]

---

notation.

[7]Here's the proof. Fix an arbitrary constant $c > 0$. In response, choose n_0 to be $\frac{1}{c}$, rounded up to the nearest integer. Then for all $n \geq n_0$, $n_0 \cdot n^{k-1} \leq n^k$ and hence $n^{k-1} \leq \frac{1}{n_0} \cdot n^k \leq c \cdot n^k$, as required.

[8]SIGACT is the special interest group of the ACM (Association for Computing Machinery) that concerns theoretical computer science, and in particular the analysis of algorithms.

[9]Donald E. Knuth, "Big Omicron and Big Omega and Big Theta," *SIGACT News*, Apr.-June 1976, page 23. Reprinted in *Selected Papers on Analysis of Algorithms* (Center for the Study of Language and Information, 2000).

2.4.5   Solution to Quiz 2.5

Correct answers: (b),(c),(d). The final three responses are all correct, and hopefully the intuition for why is clear. $T(n)$ is a quadratic function. The linear term $3n$ doesn't matter for large n, so we should expect that $T(n) = \Theta(n^2)$ (answer (c)). This automatically implies that $T(n) = \Omega(n^2)$ and hence $T(n) = \Omega(n)$ also (answer (b)). Note that $\Omega(n)$ is not a particularly impressive lower bound on $T(n)$, but it is a legitimate one nonetheless. Similarly, $T(n) = \Theta(n^2)$ implies that $T(n) = O(n^2)$ and hence also $T(n) = O(n^3)$ (answer (d)). Proving these statements formally boils down to exhibiting appropriate constants to satisfy the definitions. For example, taking $n_0 = 1$ and $c = \frac{1}{2}$ proves (b). Taking $n_0 = 1$ and $c = 4$ proves (d). Combining these constants ($n_0 = 1$, $c_1 = \frac{1}{2}$, $c_2 = 4$) proves (c). The argument in the proof of Proposition 2.2 can be used to prove formally that (a) is not a correct answer.

2.5   Additional Examples

This section is for readers who want additional practice with asymptotic notation. Other readers can skip the three additional examples here and proceed straight to Chapter 3.

2.5.1   Adding a Constant to an Exponent

First we have another example of a proof that one function is big-O of another.

Proposition 2.3 *If*

$$T(n) = 2^{n+10},$$

then $T(n) = O(2^n)$.

That is, adding a constant to the exponent of an exponential function does not change its asymptotic rate of growth.

Proof of Proposition 2.3: To satisfy the mathematical definition of big-O notation (Section 2.2.3), we just need to exhibit a suitable pair of positive constants c and n_0 (each independent of n), such that $T(n)$ is at most $c \cdot 2^n$ for all $n \geq n_0$. In the proof of Proposition 2.1 we just pulled these two constants out of a hat; here, let's reverse engineer them.

We're looking for a derivation that begins with $T(n)$ on the left-hand side, followed by a sequence of only-larger numbers, culminating in a constant multiple of 2^n. How would such a derivation begin? The "10" in the exponent is annoying, so a natural first step is to separate it out:

$$T(n) = 2^{n+10} = 2^{10} \cdot 2^n = 1024 \cdot 2^n.$$

Now we're in good shape; the right-hand side is a constant multiple of 2^n, and the derivation suggests that we should take $c = 1024$. Given this choice of c, we have $T(n) \leq c \cdot 2^n$ for all $n \geq 1$, so we just take $n_0 = 1$. This pair of constants certifies that $T(n)$ is indeed $O(2^n)$. *QED*

2.5.2   Multiplying an Exponent by a Constant

Next is another non-example, showing that one function is *not* big-O of another.

Proposition 2.4 *If*

$$T(n) = 2^{10n},$$

then $T(n)$ is not $O(2^n)$.

That is, multiplying the exponent of an exponential function by a constant changes its asymptotic rate of growth.

Proof of Proposition 2.4: As with Proposition 2.2, the usual way to prove that one function is not big-O of another is by contradiction. So assume the opposite of the statement in the proposition, that $T(n)$ is in fact $O(2^n)$. By the definition of big-O notation, this means there are positive constants c and n_0 such that

$$2^{10n} \leq c \cdot 2^n$$

for all $n \geq n_0$. Since 2^n is a positive number, we can cancel it from both sides of this inequality to derive

$$2^{9n} \leq c$$

for all $n \geq n_0$. But this inequality is patently false: the right-hand side is a fixed constant (independent of n), while the left-hand side goes to infinity as n grows large. This shows that our assumption that $T(n) = O(2^n)$ cannot be correct, and we can conclude that 2^{10n} is not $O(2^n)$. $\mathcal{QED}$

2.5.3 Maximum vs. Sum

Our final example uses big-theta notation (Section 2.4.2), the asymptotic version of "equal to." This example shows that, asymptotically, there's no difference between taking the pointwise maximum of two nonnegative functions and taking their sum.

Proposition 2.5 *Let f and g denote functions from the positive integers to the nonnegative real numbers, and define*

$$T(n) = \max\{f(n), g(n)\}$$

for each $n \geq 1$. Then $T(n) = \Theta(f(n) + g(n))$.

One consequence of Proposition 2.5 is that an algorithm that performs a constant number (meaning independent of n) of $O(f(n))$-time subroutines runs in $O(f(n))$ time.

Proof of Proposition 2.5: Recall that $T(n) = \Theta(f(n))$ means that $T(n)$ is eventually sandwiched between two different constant multiples of $f(n)$. To make this precise, we need to exhibit three constants: the usual constant n_0, and the constants c_1 and c_2 corresponding to the smaller and larger multiples of $f(n)$. Let's reverse engineer values for these constants.

Consider an arbitrary positive integer n. We have

$$\max\{f(n), g(n)\} \leq f(n) + g(n),$$

since the right-hand side is just the left-hand side plus a nonnegative number ($f(n)$ or $g(n)$, whichever is smaller). Similarly,

$$2 \cdot \max\{f(n), g(n)\} \geq f(n) + g(n),$$

since the left-hand side is two copies of the larger of $f(n), g(n)$ and the right-hand side is one copy of each. Putting these two inequalities together, we see that

$$\frac{1}{2}\left(f(n) + g(n)\right) \leq \max\{f(n), g(n)\} \leq f(n) + g(n) \qquad (2.3)$$

for every $n \geq 1$. Thus $\max\{f(n), g(n)\}$ is indeed wedged between two different multiples of $f(n) + g(n)$. Formally, choosing $n_0 = 1$, $c_1 = \frac{1}{2}$, and $c_2 = 1$ shows (by (2.3)) that $\max\{f(n), g(n)\} = \Theta(f(n) + g(n))$. $\mathscr{QED}$

The Upshot

☆ The purpose of asymptotic notation is to suppress constant factors (which are too system-dependent) and lower-order terms (which are irrelevant for large inputs).

☆ A function $T(n)$ is said to be "big-O of $f(n)$," written "$T(n) = O(f(n))$," if it is eventually (for sufficiently large n) bounded above by a constant multiple of $f(n)$. That is, there are positive constants c and n_0 such that $T(n) \leq c \cdot f(n)$ for all $n \geq n_0$.

☆ A function $T(n)$ is "big-omega of $f(n)$," written "$T(n) = \Omega(f(n))$," if it is eventually bounded below by a constant multiple of $f(n)$.

☆ A function $T(n)$ is "big-theta of $f(n)$," written "$T(n) = \Theta(f(n))$," if both $T(n) = O(f(n))$ and $T(n) = \Omega(f(n))$.

☆ A big-O statement is analogous to "less than or equal to," big-omega to "greater than or equal to," and big-theta to "equal to."

Test Your Understanding

Problem 2.1 *(S)* Let f and g be non-decreasing real-valued functions defined on the positive integers, with $f(n)$ and $g(n)$ at least 1 for all $n \geq 1$. Assume that $f(n) = O(g(n))$, and let c be a positive constant. Is $f(n) \cdot \log_2(f(n)^c) = O(g(n) \cdot \log_2(g(n)))$?

  a) Yes, for all such f, g, and c

b) Never, no matter what f, g, and c are

c) Sometimes yes, sometimes no, depending on the constant c

d) Sometimes yes, sometimes no, depending on the functions f and g

Problem 2.2 Assume again two positive non-decreasing functions f and g such that $f(n) = O(g(n))$. Is $2^{f(n)} = O(2^{g(n)})$? (Multiple answers may be correct; choose all that apply.)

a) Yes, for all such f and g

b) Never, no matter what f and g are

c) Sometimes yes, sometimes no, depending on the functions f and g

d) Yes whenever $f(n) \leq g(n)$ for all sufficiently large n

Problem 2.3 Arrange the following functions in order of increasing growth rate, with $g(n)$ following $f(n)$ in your list if and only if $f(n) = O(g(n))$.

a) $\sqrt{n}$

b) 10^n

c) $n^{1.5}$

d) $2^{\sqrt{\log_2 n}}$

e) $n^{5/3}$

Problem 2.4 Arrange the following functions in order of increasing growth rate, with $g(n)$ following $f(n)$ in your list if and only if $f(n) = O(g(n))$.

a) $n^2 \log_2 n$

b) 2^n

c) 2^{2^n}

d) $n^{\log_2 n}$

e) n^2

Problem 2.5 *(S)* Arrange the following functions in order of increasing growth rate, with $g(n)$ following $f(n)$ in your list if and only if $f(n) = O(g(n))$.

a) $2^{\log_2 n}$

b) $2^{2^{\log_2 n}}$

c) $n^{5/2}$

d) 2^{n^2}

e) $n^2 \log_2 n$

Chapter 3

Divide-and-Conquer Algorithms

This chapter provides practice with the divide-and-conquer algorithm design paradigm through applications to three basic problems. Our first example is an algorithm for counting the number of inversions in an array (Section 3.2). This problem is related to measuring similarity between two ranked lists, which is relevant for making good recommendations to someone based on your knowledge of their and others' preferences (called "collaborative filtering"). Our second divide-and-conquer algorithm is Strassen's mind-blowing recursive algorithm for matrix multiplication, which improves over the obvious iterative method (Section 3.3). The third algorithm, which is advanced and optional material, is for a fundamental problem in computational geometry: computing the closest pair of points in the plane (Section 3.4).[1]

3.1 The Divide-and-Conquer Paradigm

You've seen the canonical example of a divide-and-conquer algorithm, `MergeSort` (Section 1.4). More generally, the divide-and-conquer algorithm design paradigm has three conceptual steps.

The Divide-and-Conquer Paradigm

1. *Divide* the input into smaller subproblems.

2. *Conquer* the subproblems recursively.

3. *Combine* the solutions for the subproblems into a solution for the original problem.

---

[1]The presentation in Sections 3.2 and 3.4 draws inspiration from Chapter 5 of *Algorithm Design*, by Jon Kleinberg and Éva Tardos (Pearson, 2005).

For example, in MergeSort, the "divide" step splits the input array into its left and right halves, the "conquer" step uses two recursive calls to sort the left and right subarrays, and the "combine" step is implemented by the Merge subroutine (Section 1.4.5). In MergeSort and many other algorithms, it is the last step that requires the most ingenuity. There are also divide-and-conquer algorithms in which the cleverness is in the first step (see QuickSort in Chapter 5) or in the specification of the recursive calls (see Section 3.2).

3.2   Counting Inversions in $O(n \log n)$ Time

3.2.1   The Problem

This section studies the problem of computing the number of inversions in an array. An *inversion* of an array is a pair of elements that are "out of order," meaning that the element that occurs earlier in the array is bigger than the one that occurs later.

Problem: Counting Inversions

Input: An array A of distinct integers.

Output: The number of inversions of A—the number of pairs (i, j) of array indices with $i < j$ and $A[i] > A[j]$.

For example, an array A that is in sorted order has no inversions. You should convince yourself that the converse is also true: every array that is not in sorted order has at least one inversion.

3.2.2   An Example

Consider the following array of length 6:

1	3	5	2	4	6

How many inversions does this array have? One that jumps out is the 5 and 2 (corresponding to $i = 3$ and $j = 4$). There are exactly two other out-of-order pairs: the 3 and the 2, and the 5 and the 4.

Quiz 3.1

What is the largest-possible number of inversions a 6-element array can have?

    a) 15

    b) 21

    c) 36

    d) 64

(See Section 3.2.13 for the solution and discussion.)

3.2.3   Collaborative Filtering

Why would you want to count the number of inversions in an array? One reason is to compute a numerical similarity measure that quantifies how close two ranked lists are to each other. For example, suppose I ask you and a friend to rank, from favorite to least favorite, ten movies that you have both seen. Are your tastes "similar" or "different?" One way to answer this question quantitatively is through the following 10-element array A: $A[1]$ contains your friend's ranking of your favorite movie in their list, $A[2]$ your friend's personal ranking of your second-favorite movie, ..., and $A[10]$ your friend's personal ranking of your least favorite movie. So if your favorite movie is *Star Wars* but your friend has it only fifth in their list, then $A[1] = 5$. If your rankings are identical, this array will be sorted and have no inversions. The more inversions the array has, the more pairs of movies on which you disagree about their relative merits, and the more different your preferences.

One reason you might want a similarity measure between rankings is to do *collaborative filtering*, a technique for generating recommendations. How do Web sites come up with suggestions for products, movies, songs, news stories, and so on? In collaborative filtering, the idea is to identify other users who have similar preferences, and to recommend to you things that have been popular with them. Thus collaborative filtering algorithms require a formal notion of "similarity" between users, and the problem of computing inversions captures some of the essence of this problem.

3.2.4   Brute-Force Search

How quickly can we compute the number of inversions in an array? If we're feeling unimaginative, there's always brute-force search.

Brute-Force Search for Counting Inversions

Input: array A of n distinct integers.
Output: the number of inversions of A.

$numInv := 0$
for $i := 1$ to $n - 1$ **do**
    for $j := i + 1$ to n **do**
        if $A[i] > A[j]$ **then**
            $numInv := numInv + 1$
    return $numInv$

This is certainly a correct algorithm. What about its running time? From the solution to Quiz 3.1, we know that the number of loop iterations grows quadratically with the length n of the input array. Since the algorithm does a constant number of operations in each loop iteration, its asymptotic running time is $\Theta(n^2)$. Remember the mantra of a seasoned algorithm designer: *can we do better?*

3.2.5   A Divide-and-Conquer Approach

The answer is yes, and the solution will be a divide-and-conquer algorithm that runs in $O(n \log n)$ time, a big improvement over the brute-force search algorithm. The "divide" step will be exactly as in the MergeSort algorithm, with one recursive call for the left half of the array and one for the right half. To understand the residual work that needs to be done outside the two recursive calls, let's classify the inversions (i, j) of an array A of length n into one of three types:

1. *left inversion*: an inversion with i, j both in the first half of the array (i.e., $i, j \leq \frac{n}{2}$);[2]

---

[2]The abbreviation "i.e." stands for *id est*, and means "that is."

2. *right inversion*: an inversion with i, j both in the second half of the array (i.e., $i, j > \frac{n}{2}$);

3. *split inversion*: an inversion with i in the left half and j in the right half (i.e., $i \leq \frac{n}{2} < j$).

For example, in the six-element array in Section 3.2.2, all three of the inversions are split inversions.

The first recursive call, on the first half of the input array, recursively counts all the left inversions (and nothing else). Similarly, the second recursive call counts all the right inversions. The remaining task is to count the inversions not counted by either recursive call—the split inversions. This is the "combine" step of the algorithm, and we will need to implement a special linear-time subroutine for it, analogous to the `Merge` subroutine in the `MergeSort` algorithm.

3.2.6   High-Level Algorithm

Our divide-and-conquer approach translates to the following pseudocode; the subroutine `CountSplitInv` is, as of now, unimplemented.

CountInv

Input: array A of n distinct integers.
Output: the number of inversions of A.

---

if $n = 0$ or $n = 1$ **then**   // base cases
    return 0
else
    $leftInv := $ `CountInv`(first half of A)
    $rightInv := $ `CountInv`(second half of A)
    $splitInv := $ `CountSplitInv`(A)
    return $leftInv + rightInv + splitInv$

The first and second recursive calls count the number of left and right inversions. Provided the subroutine `CountSplitInv` correctly computes the number of split inversions, `CountInv` correctly computes the total number of inversions.

3.2.7   Key Idea: Piggyback on MergeSort

Counting the number of split inversions of an array in linear time is an ambitious goal. There can be a lot of split inversions: if A consists of the numbers $\frac{n}{2} + 1, \ldots, n$ in order, followed by the numbers $1, 2, \ldots, \frac{n}{2}$ in order, there are $n^2/4$ split inversions. How could we ever count a quadratic number of things with only a linear amount of work?

The inspired idea is to design our recursive inversion-counting algorithm so that it piggybacks on the MergeSort algorithm. This involves demanding more from our recursive calls, in service of making it easier to count the number of split inversions.[3] Each recursive call will be responsible not only for counting the number of inversions in the array that it is given, but also for returning a sorted version of the array. We already know (from Theorem 1.2) that sorting is a for-free primitive (see page 31), running in $O(n \log n)$ time, so if we're shooting for a running time bound of $O(n \log n)$, there's no reason not to sort. And we'll see that the task of merging two sorted subarrays is tailor-made for uncovering all the split inversions of an array.

Here is the revised version of the pseudocode in Section 3.2.6, which counts inversions while also sorting the input array.

Sort-and-CountInv

Input: array A of n distinct integers.
Output: sorted array B with the same integers, and the number of inversions of A.

---

if $n = 0$ or $n = 1$ **then**   // base cases
    return $(A, 0)$
else
    $(C, leftInv) :=$
      Sort-and-CountInv(first half of A)
    $(D, rightInv) :=$
      Sort-and-CountInv(second half of A)
    $(B, splitInv) :=$ Merge-and-CountSplitInv(C, D)
    return $(B, leftInv + rightInv + splitInv)$

---

[3]Similarly, sometimes a proof by induction becomes easier to push through after strengthening your inductive hypothesis.

We still need to implement the `Merge-and-CountSplitInv` subroutine. We know how to merge two sorted lists in linear time, but how can we piggyback on this work to also count the number of split inversions?

3.2.8   Merge Revisited

To see why merging sorted subarrays naturally uncovers split inversions, let's revisit the pseudocode for the `Merge` subroutine.

Merge

Input: sorted arrays C and D (length $n/2$ each).
Output: sorted array B (length n).
Simplifying assumption: n is even.

$i := 1$, $j := 1$
for $k := 1$ **to** n **do**
    if $C[i] < D[j]$ **then**
        $B[k] := C[i]$, $i := i + 1$
    else   // $D[j] < C[i]$
        $B[k] := D[j]$, $j := j + 1$

To review, the `Merge` subroutine walks one index down each of the sorted subarrays in parallel (i for C and j for D), populating the output array (B) from left to right in sorted order (using the index k). At each iteration of the loop, the subroutine identifies the smallest element that it hasn't yet copied over to B. Since C and D are sorted, and all the elements before $C[i]$ and $D[j]$ have already been copied over to B, the only two candidates are $C[i]$ and $D[j]$. The subroutine determines which of the two is smaller and then copies it over to the next position of the output array.

What does the `Merge` subroutine have to do with counting the number of split inversions? Let's start with the special case of an array A that has no split inversions at all—every inversion of A is either a left or a right inversion.

Quiz 3.2

Suppose the input array A has no split inversions. What is the relationship between the sorted subarrays C and D?

a) C has the smallest element of A, D the second-smallest, C the third-smallest, and so on.

b) All elements of C are less than all elements of D.

c) All elements of C are greater than all elements of D.

d) There is not enough information to answer this question.

(See Section 3.2.13 for the solution and discussion.)

After solving Quiz 3.2, you can see that Merge has an particularly boring execution on an array with no split inversions. Since every element of C is smaller than every element of D, the smallest remaining element is always in C (until no elements of C remain). Thus the Merge subroutine just concatenates C and D—it will first copy over all of C, and then all of D. This suggests that, perhaps, split inversions have something to do with the number of elements remaining in C when an element of D is copied over to the output array.

3.2.9   Merge and Split Inversions

To build our intuition further, let's think about running the MergeSort algorithm on the six-element array $A = \{1, 3, 5, 2, 4, 6\}$ from Section 3.2.2; see also Figure 3.1. The left and right halves of this array are already sorted, so there are no left inversions or right inversions, and the two recursive calls return 0. In the first iteration of the Merge subroutine, the first element of C (the 1) is copied over to B. This tells us nothing about any split inversions, and indeed there are no split inversions that involve this element. In the second iteration, however, the 2 is copied over to the output array, even though C still contains the elements 3 and 5. This exposes two of the split inversions of A—the two such inversions that involve the 2. In the third iteration, the 3 is copied over from C and there are no further split inversions that involve this element. When the 4 is copied over from D, the array C still contains a 5, and this copy exposes the third and final split inversion of A (involving the 5 and the 4).

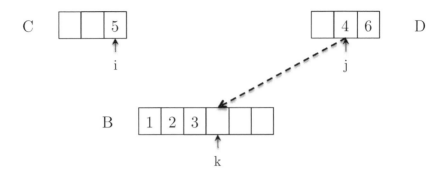

Figure 3.1: The fourth iteration of the Merge subroutine given the sorted subarrays $\{1, 3, 5\}$ and $\{2, 4, 6\}$. Copying the 4 over from D, with the 5 still in C, exposes the split inversion involving these two elements.

The following lemma states that the pattern in the example above holds in general: the number of split inversions that involve an element y of the second subarray D is precisely the number of elements remaining in C in the iteration of the Merge subroutine in which y is copied to the output array.

Lemma 3.1 *Let A be an array, and C and D sorted versions of the first and second halves of A. An element x from the first half of A and y from the second half of A form a split inversion if and only if, in the Merge subroutine with inputs C and D, y is copied to the output array before x.*

Proof: Since the output array is populated from left to right in sorted order, the smaller of x or y is copied over first. Since x is in the first half of A and y in the second half, x and y form a split inversion if and only if $x > y$, and this is true if and only if y is copied over to the output array before x. *QED*

3.2.10   Merge-and-CountSplitInv

With the insight provided by Lemma 3.1, we can extend the implementation of Merge to an implementation of Merge-and-CountSplitInv. We maintain a running count of the split inversions, and every time an element is copied over from the second subarray D to the output array B, we increment the running count by the number of elements remaining in the first subarray C.

Merge-and-CountSplitInv

Input: sorted arrays C and D (length $n/2$ each).
Output: sorted array B (length n) and the number of split inversions.
Simplifying assumption: n is even.

$i := 1$, $j := 1$, $splitInv := 0$
for $k := 1$ to n **do**
    if $C[i] < D[j]$ **then**
        $B[k] := C[i]$, $i := i + 1$
    else   // $D[j] < C[i]$
        $B[k] := D[j]$, $j := j + 1$
        $splitInv := splitInv + \underbrace{\left(\tfrac{n}{2} - i + 1\right)}_{\#\text{ left in } C}$
return $(B, splitInv)$

3.2.11   Correctness

Correctness of `Merge-and-CountSplitInv` follows from Lemma 3.1. Every split inversion involves exactly one element y from the second subarray, and this inversion is counted exactly once, when y is copied over to the output array. Correctness of the entire `Sort-and-CountInv` algorithm (Section 3.2.7) follows: the first recursive call correctly computes the number of left inversions, the second recursive call the number of right inversions, and `Merge-and-CountSplitInv` the remaining (split) inversions.

3.2.12   Running Time

We can also analyze the running time of the `Sort-and-CountInv` algorithm by piggybacking on the analysis we already did for the `MergeSort` algorithm. First consider the running time of a single invocation of the `Merge-and-CountSplitInv` subroutine, given two subarrays of length $\ell/2$ each. Like the `Merge` subroutine, it does a constant number of operations per loop iteration, plus a constant number of additional operations, for a running time of $O(\ell)$.

Looking back at our running time analysis of the `MergeSort` algorithm in Section 1.5, we can see that there were three important properties of the algorithm that led to the running time bound of $O(n \log n)$. First, each invocation of the algorithm makes two recursive calls. Second, the length of the input is divided in half with each level of recursion. Third, the amount of work done in a recursive call, not counting work done by later recursive calls, is linear in the input size. Since the `Sort-and-CountInv` algorithm shares these three properties, the analysis in Section 1.5 carries over, again giving a running time bound of $O(n \log n)$.

Theorem 3.2 (Counting Inversions) *For every input array A of length $n \geq 1$, the `Sort-and-CountInv` algorithm computes the number of inversions of A and runs in $O(n \log n)$ time.*

3.2.13   Solutions to Quizzes 3.1–3.2

Solution to Quiz 3.1

Correct answer: (a). The correct answer to this question is 15. The maximum-possible number of inversions is at most the number of ways of choosing $i, j \in \{1, 2, \ldots, 6\}$ with $i < j$. The latter quantity is denoted $\binom{6}{2}$, for "6 choose 2." In general, $\binom{n}{2} = \frac{n(n-1)}{2}$, and so $\binom{6}{2} = 15$.[4] In a six-element array sorted in reverse order $(6, 5, \ldots, 1)$, every pair of elements is out of order, and so this array achieves 15 inversions.

Solution to Quiz 3.2

Correct answer: (b). In an array with no split inversions, everything in the first half is less than everything in the second half. If there *was* an element $A[i]$ in the first half (with $i \in \{1, 2, \ldots, \frac{n}{2}\}$) that is greater than an element $A[j]$ in the second half (with $j \in \{\frac{n}{2}+1, \frac{n}{2}+2, \ldots, n\}$), then (i, j) would constitute a split inversion.

---

[4]There are $n(n-1)$ ways to choose (i, j) so that $i \neq j$ (n choices for i, then $n-1$ for j). By symmetry, $i < j$ in exactly half of these.

3.3   Strassen's Matrix Multiplication Algorithm

This section applies the divide-and-conquer algorithm design paradigm
to the problem of multiplying matrices, culminating in Strassen's amazing subcubic-time matrix multiplication algorithm. This algorithm
is a canonical example of the magic and power of clever algorithm
design—of how algorithmic ingenuity can improve over straightforward
solutions, even for extremely fundamental problems.

3.3.1   Matrix Multiplication

Suppose $\mathbf{X}$ and $\mathbf{Y}$ are $n \times n$ matrices of integers—n^2 entries in each.
In the product $\mathbf{Z} = \mathbf{X} \cdot \mathbf{Y}$, the entry z_{ij} in the ith row and jth column
of $\mathbf{Z}$ is defined as the dot product of the ith row of $\mathbf{X}$ and the jth
column of $\mathbf{Y}$ (Figure 3.2).[5] That is,

$$z_{ij} = \sum_{k=1}^{n} x_{ik} y_{kj}. \tag{3.1}$$

Figure 3.2: The (i, j) entry of the matrix product $\mathbf{X} \cdot \mathbf{Y}$ is the dot product
of the ith row of $\mathbf{X}$ and the jth column of $\mathbf{Y}$.

3.3.2   Example ($n = 2$)

Let's drill down on the $n = 2$ case. We can describe two 2×2 matrices
using eight parameters:

$$\underbrace{\begin{pmatrix} a & b \\ c & d \end{pmatrix}}_{\mathbf{X}} \quad \text{and} \quad \underbrace{\begin{pmatrix} e & f \\ g & h \end{pmatrix}}_{\mathbf{Y}}.$$

---

[5]To compute the *dot product* of two length-n vectors $\mathbf{a} = (a_1, \ldots, a_n)$ and $\mathbf{b} = (b_1, \ldots, b_n)$, add up the results of multiplying componentwise: $\mathbf{a} \cdot \mathbf{b} = \sum_{i=1}^{n} a_i b_i$.

In the matrix product $\mathbf{X} \cdot \mathbf{Y}$, the upper-left entry is the dot product of the first row of $\mathbf{X}$ and the first column of $\mathbf{Y}$, or $ae + bg$. In general, for $\mathbf{X}$ and $\mathbf{Y}$ as above,

$$\mathbf{X} \cdot \mathbf{Y} = \left(\begin{array}{cc} ae + bg & af + bh \\ ce + dg & cf + dh \end{array} \right). \tag{3.2}$$

3.3.3   The Straightforward Algorithm

Now let's think about algorithms for computing the product of two matrices.

Problem: Matrix Multiplication

Input: Two $n \times n$ integer matrices, $\mathbf{X}$ and $\mathbf{Y}$.[6]

Output: The matrix product $\mathbf{X} \cdot \mathbf{Y}$.

The input size is proportional to n^2, the number of entries in each of $\mathbf{X}$ and $\mathbf{Y}$. Since we presumably have to read the input and write out the output, the best we can hope for is an algorithm with running time $O(n^2)$—linear in the input size, and quadratic in the dimension. How close can we get to this best-case scenario?

There is a straightforward algorithm for matrix multiplication, which just translates the mathematical definition into code.

Straightforward Matrix Multiplication

Input: $n \times n$ integer matrices $\mathbf{X}$ and $\mathbf{Y}$.
Output: $\mathbf{Z} = \mathbf{X} \cdot \mathbf{Y}$.

---

for $i := 1$ to n **do**
   for $j := 1$ to n **do**
      $\mathbf{Z}[i][j] := 0$
      for $k := 1$ to n **do**
         $\mathbf{Z}[i][j] := \mathbf{Z}[i][j] + \mathbf{X}[i][k] \cdot \mathbf{Y}[k][j]$
   return $\mathbf{Z}$

---

[6]The algorithms we discuss can also be extended to multiply non-square matrices, but we'll stick with the square case for simplicity.

What is the running time of this algorithm?

Quiz 3.3

What is the asymptotic running time of the straightforward algorithm for matrix multiplication, as a function of the matrix dimension n? Assume that the addition or multiplication of two matrix entries is a constant-time operation.

  a) $\Theta(n \log n)$

  b) $\Theta(n^2)$

  c) $\Theta(n^3)$

  d) $\Theta(n^4)$

(See Section 3.3.7 for the solution and discussion.)

3.3.4   A Divide-and-Conquer Approach

The question is, as always, *can we do better?* Everyone's first reaction is that matrix multiplication should, essentially by definition, require $\Omega(n^3)$ time. But perhaps we're emboldened by the success of the `Karatsuba` algorithm for integer multiplication (Section 1.3), where a clever divide-and-conquer algorithm improves over the straightforward grade-school algorithm.[7] Could a similar approach work for multiplying matrices?

To apply the divide-and-conquer paradigm (Section 3.1), we need to figure out how to divide the input into smaller subproblems and how to combine the solutions of these subproblems into a solution for the original problem. The simplest way to divide a square matrix into smaller square submatrices is to slice it in half, both vertically and horizontally. In other words, write

$$\mathbf{X} = \begin{pmatrix} \mathbf{A} & \mathbf{B} \\ \mathbf{C} & \mathbf{D} \end{pmatrix} \quad \text{and} \quad \mathbf{Y} = \begin{pmatrix} \mathbf{E} & \mathbf{F} \\ \mathbf{G} & \mathbf{H} \end{pmatrix}, \qquad (3.3)$$

where $\mathbf{A}, \mathbf{B}, \dots, \mathbf{H}$ are all $\frac{n}{2} \times \frac{n}{2}$ matrices.[8]

---

[7]We haven't actually proved this yet, but we will in Section 4.3.

[8]As usual, we're assuming that n is even for convenience. And as usual, it doesn't really matter.

One cool thing about matrix multiplication is that equal-size blocks behave just like individual entries. That is, for $\mathbf{X}$ and $\mathbf{Y}$ as above, we have

$$\mathbf{X} \cdot \mathbf{Y} = \left(\begin{array}{cc} \mathbf{A} \cdot \mathbf{E} + \mathbf{B} \cdot \mathbf{G} & \mathbf{A} \cdot \mathbf{F} + \mathbf{B} \cdot \mathbf{H} \\ \mathbf{C} \cdot \mathbf{E} + \mathbf{D} \cdot \mathbf{G} & \mathbf{C} \cdot \mathbf{F} + \mathbf{D} \cdot \mathbf{H} \end{array} \right), \qquad (3.4)$$

completely analogous to the equation (3.2) for the $n = 2$ case. (This follows from the definition of matrix multiplication, as you should check.) In (3.4), adding two matrices just means adding them entrywise—the (i, j) entry of $\mathbf{K} + \mathbf{L}$ is the sum of the (i, j) entries of $\mathbf{K}$ and $\mathbf{L}$. The decomposition and computation in (3.4) translates naturally to a recursive algorithm for matrix multiplication, RecMatMult.

RecMatMult

Input: $n \times n$ integer matrices $\mathbf{X}$ and $\mathbf{Y}$.
Output: $\mathbf{Z} = \mathbf{X} \cdot \mathbf{Y}$.
Assumption: n is a power of 2.

---

if $n = 1$ then   // base case
    return the 1×1 matrix with entry $\mathbf{X}[1][1] \cdot \mathbf{Y}[1][1]$
else   // recursive case
    $\mathbf{A}, \mathbf{B}, \mathbf{C}, \mathbf{D} :=$ submatrices of $\mathbf{X}$ as in (3.3)
    $\mathbf{E}, \mathbf{F}, \mathbf{G}, \mathbf{H} :=$ submatrices of $\mathbf{Y}$ as in (3.3)
    recursively compute the eight matrix products that
      appear in (3.4)
    return the result of the computation in (3.4)

The running time of the RecMatMult algorithm is not immediately obvious. What is clear is that there are eight recursive calls, each on an input of half the dimension. Other than making these recursive calls, the only work required is the matrix additions in (3.4). Since an $n \times n$ matrix has n^2 entries, and the number of operations needed to add two matrices is proportional to the number of entries, a recursive call on a pair of $\ell \times \ell$ matrices performs $\Theta(\ell^2)$ operations, not counting the work done by its own recursive calls.

Disappointingly, this recursive algorithm turns out to have a running time of $\Theta(n^3)$, the same as the straightforward algorithm.

(This follows from the "master method," explained in the next chapter.) Has all our work been for naught? Remember that in the integer multiplication problem, the key to beating the grade-school algorithm was Gauss's trick, which reduced the number of recursive calls from four to three (Section 1.3.3). Is there an analog of Gauss's trick for matrix multiplication, one that allows us to reduce the number of recursive calls from eight to seven?

3.3.5   Saving a Recursive Call

The high-level plan of the `Strassen` algorithm is to save one recursive call relative to the `RecMatMult` algorithm, in exchange for a constant number of additional matrix additions and subtractions.

Strassen (Very High-Level Description)

Input: $n \times n$ integer matrices $\mathbf{X}$ and $\mathbf{Y}$.
Output: $\mathbf{Z} = \mathbf{X} \cdot \mathbf{Y}$.
Assumption: n is a power of 2.

---

if $n = 1$ then   // base case
    return the 1×1 matrix with entry $\mathbf{X}[1][1] \cdot \mathbf{Y}[1][1]$
else   // recursive case
    $\mathbf{A}, \mathbf{B}, \mathbf{C}, \mathbf{D} :=$ submatrices of $\mathbf{X}$ as in (3.3)
    $\mathbf{E}, \mathbf{F}, \mathbf{G}, \mathbf{H} :=$ submatrices of $\mathbf{Y}$ as in (3.3)
    recursively compute seven (cleverly chosen)
      products involving $\mathbf{A}, \mathbf{B}, \ldots, \mathbf{H}$
    return the appropriate (cleverly chosen) additions
      and subtractions of the matrices computed in the
      previous step

Saving one of the eight recursive calls is a big win. It doesn't merely reduce the running time of the algorithm by 12.5%. The recursive call is saved over and over again, so the savings are compounded and—spoiler alert!—this results in an asymptotically superior running time. We'll see the exact running time bound in Section 4.3, but for now the important thing to know is that saving a recursive call yields an algorithm with subcubic running time.

This concludes all the high-level points you should know about Strassen's matrix multiplication algorithm. Are you in disbelief that it's possible to improve over the obvious algorithm? Or curious about exactly how the products and additions are actually chosen? If so, the next section is for you.

3.3.6   The Details

Let $\mathbf{X}$ and $\mathbf{Y}$ denote the two $n \times n$ input matrices, and define $\mathbf{A}, \mathbf{B}, \ldots, \mathbf{H}$ as in (3.3). Here are the seven recursive matrix multiplications performed by Strassen's algorithm:

$$\mathbf{P}_1 = \mathbf{A} \cdot (\mathbf{F} - \mathbf{H})$$
$$\mathbf{P}_2 = (\mathbf{A} + \mathbf{B}) \cdot \mathbf{H}$$
$$\mathbf{P}_3 = (\mathbf{C} + \mathbf{D}) \cdot \mathbf{E}$$
$$\mathbf{P}_4 = \mathbf{D} \cdot (\mathbf{G} - \mathbf{E})$$
$$\mathbf{P}_5 = (\mathbf{A} + \mathbf{D}) \cdot (\mathbf{E} + \mathbf{H})$$
$$\mathbf{P}_6 = (\mathbf{B} - \mathbf{D}) \cdot (\mathbf{G} + \mathbf{H})$$
$$\mathbf{P}_7 = (\mathbf{A} - \mathbf{C}) \cdot (\mathbf{E} + \mathbf{F}).$$

After spending $\Theta(n^2)$ time performing the necessary matrix additions and subtractions, $\mathbf{P}_1, \ldots, \mathbf{P}_7$ can be computed using seven recursive calls on pairs of $\frac{n}{2} \times \frac{n}{2}$ matrices. But is this really enough information to reconstruct the matrix product of $\mathbf{X}$ and $\mathbf{Y}$ in $\Theta(n^2)$ time? The following amazing equation gives an affirmative answer:

$$\mathbf{X} \cdot \mathbf{Y} = \left(\begin{array}{c|c} \mathbf{A} \cdot \mathbf{E} + \mathbf{B} \cdot \mathbf{G} & \mathbf{A} \cdot \mathbf{F} + \mathbf{B} \cdot \mathbf{H} \\ \hline \mathbf{C} \cdot \mathbf{E} + \mathbf{D} \cdot \mathbf{G} & \mathbf{C} \cdot \mathbf{F} + \mathbf{D} \cdot \mathbf{H} \end{array} \right)$$
$$= \left(\begin{array}{c|c} \mathbf{P}_5 + \mathbf{P}_4 - \mathbf{P}_2 + \mathbf{P}_6 & \mathbf{P}_1 + \mathbf{P}_2 \\ \hline \mathbf{P}_3 + \mathbf{P}_4 & \mathbf{P}_1 + \mathbf{P}_5 - \mathbf{P}_3 - \mathbf{P}_7 \end{array} \right).$$

The first equation is copied from (3.4). For the second equation, we need to check that the equality holds in each of the four quadrants. To quell your disbelief, check out the crazy cancellations in the upper-left quadrant:

$$
\begin{aligned}
\mathbf{P}_5 + \mathbf{P}_4 - \mathbf{P}_2 + \mathbf{P}_6 = \quad & (\mathbf{A} + \mathbf{D}) \cdot (\mathbf{E} + \mathbf{H}) + \mathbf{D} \cdot (\mathbf{G} - \mathbf{E}) \\
& - (\mathbf{A} + \mathbf{B}) \cdot \mathbf{H} + (\mathbf{B} - \mathbf{D}) \cdot (\mathbf{G} + \mathbf{H}) \\
= \quad & \mathbf{A} \cdot \mathbf{E} + \mathbf{A} \cdot \mathbf{H} + \mathbf{D} \cdot \mathbf{E} + \mathbf{D} \cdot \mathbf{H} + \mathbf{D} \cdot \mathbf{G} \\
& - \mathbf{D} \cdot \mathbf{E} - \mathbf{A} \cdot \mathbf{H} - \mathbf{B} \cdot \mathbf{H} + \mathbf{B} \cdot \mathbf{G} \\
& + \mathbf{B} \cdot \mathbf{H} - \mathbf{D} \cdot \mathbf{G} - \mathbf{D} \cdot \mathbf{H} \\
= \quad & \mathbf{A} \cdot \mathbf{E} + \mathbf{B} \cdot \mathbf{G}.
\end{aligned}
$$

The computation for the lower-right quadrant is similar, and equality is easy to see in the other two quadrants. So the `Strassen` algorithm really can multiply matrices with only seven recursive calls and $\Theta(n^2)$ additional work![9]

3.3.7   Solution to Quiz 3.3

Correct answer: (c). The correct answer is $\Theta(n^3)$. There are three nested for loops. This results in n^3 inner loop iterations (one for each choice of $i, j, k \in \{1, 2, \ldots, n\}$), and the algorithm performs a constant number of operations in each iteration (one multiplication and one addition). Alternatively, for each of the n^2 entries of $\mathbf{Z}$, the algorithm spends $\Theta(n)$ time evaluating (3.1).

*3.4   An $O(n \log n)$-Time Algorithm for the Closest Pair

Our final example of a divide-and-conquer algorithm is a very cool algorithm for the closest pair problem, in which you're given n points in the plane and want to figure out the pair of points that are closest to each other. This is our first taste of an application in computational geometry, an area that studies algorithms for reasoning about and

---

[9]Of course, checking that the algorithm works is a lot easier than coming up with it in the first place. And how did Volker Strassen ever come up with it, back in 1969? Here's what he said (in a personal communication, June 2017): "The way I remember it, I had realized that a faster noncommutative algorithm for some small case would give a better exponent. I tried to prove that the straightforward algorithm is optimal for 2×2 matrices. To simplify matters I worked modulo 2, and then discovered the faster algorithm combinatorially."

manipulating geometric objects, and that has applications in robotics, computer vision, and computer graphics.[10]

3.4.1   The Problem

The closest pair problem concerns points $(x, y) \in \mathbb{R}^2$ in the plane. To measure the distance between two points $p_1 = (x_1, y_1)$ and $p_2 = (x_2, y_2)$, we use the usual Euclidean (straight-line) distance:

$$d(p_1, p_2) = \sqrt{(x_1 - x_2)^2 + (y_1 - y_2)^2}. \qquad (3.5)$$

Problem: Closest Pair

Input: $n \geq 2$ points $p_1 = (x_1, y_1), \ldots, p_n = (x_n, y_n)$ in the plane.

Output: The pair p_i, p_j of points with smallest Euclidean distance $d(p_i, p_j)$.

For convenience, we'll assume that no two points have the same x-coordinate or the same y-coordinate. You should think about how to extend the algorithm from this section to accommodate ties.[11]

The closest pair problem can be solved in quadratic time using brute-force search—just compute the distance between each of the $\Theta(n^2)$ pairs of points one-by-one, and return the closest of them. For the counting inversions problem (Section 3.2), we were able to improve over the quadratic-time brute-force search algorithm with a divide-and-conquer algorithm. Can we also do better here?

3.4.2   Warm-Up: The 1-D Case

Let's first consider the simpler one-dimensional version of the problem: given n points $p_1, \ldots, p_n \in \mathbb{R}$ in arbitrary order, identify a pair that

---

[10]Starred sections like this one are the more difficult sections, and they can be skipped on a first reading.

[11]In a real-world implementation, a closest pair algorithm will not bother to compute the square root in (3.5)—the pair of points with the smallest Euclidean distance is the same as the one with the smallest squared Euclidean distance, and the latter distance is easier to compute.

minimizes the distance $|p_i - p_j|$. This special case is easy to solve in $O(n \log n)$ time using the tools that are already in our toolbox. The key observation is that, whatever the closest pair is, the two points must appear consecutively in the sorted version of the point set (Figure 3.3).

1-D Closest Pair

sort the points
use a linear scan through the sorted points to identify
  the closest pair

The first and second steps of the algorithm can be implemented in $O(n \log n)$ time (using MergeSort) and $O(n)$ time (straightforwardly), respectively, for an overall running time of $O(n \log n)$. Thus in the one-dimensional case, there is indeed an algorithm better than brute-force search.

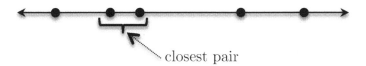

closest pair

Figure 3.3: In one dimension, the points in the closest pair appear consecutively in the sorted version of the point set.

3.4.3   Preprocessing

Can sorting help solve the two-dimensional version of the closest pair problem in $O(n \log n)$ time? An immediate issue is that there are two different coordinates you can use to sort the points. But since sorting is a for-free primitive (see page 31), why not just do it (twice)? That is, in a preprocessing step, our algorithm makes two copies of the input point set: a copy P_x with the points sorted by x-coordinate, and a copy P_y sorted by y-coordinate. This takes $O(n \log n)$ time, which is within the time bound we're shooting for.

How can we put the sorted versions P_x and P_y to use? Unfortunately, the closest pair of points need not appear consecutively in either P_x or P_y (Figure 3.4). We will have to do something more clever than a simple linear scan.

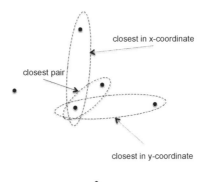

Figure 3.4: In two dimensions, the points in the closest pair need not appear consecutively when the points are sorted by x- or y-coordinate.

3.4.4   A Divide-and-Conquer Approach

We can do better with a divide-and-conquer approach.[12] How should we divide the input into smaller subproblems, and how can we then combine the solutions of these subproblems into one for the original problem? For the first question, we use the first sorted array P_x to divide the input into its left and right halves. Call a pair of points a *left pair* if both belong to the left half of the point set, a *right pair* if both belong to the right half, and a *split pair* if the points belong to different halves. For example, in the point set in Figure 3.4, the closest pair is a split pair, and the pair of points closest in x-coordinate is a left pair.

If the closest pair is a left pair or a right pair, it will be recursively identified by one of the two recursive calls. We'll need a special-purpose subroutine for the remaining case, when the closest pair is a split pair. This subroutine plays a similar role to the `CountSplitInv` subroutine in Section 3.2.

The following pseudocode summarizes these ideas; the subroutine `ClosestSplitPair` is, as of now, unimplemented.

---

[12]Thus the divide-and-conquer paradigm is used in both the preprocessing step, to implement `MergeSort`, and again in the main algorithm.

ClosestPair (Preliminary Version)

Input: two copies P_x and P_y of $n \geq 2$ points in the plane, sorted by x- and y-coordinate, respectively.
Output: the pair p_i, p_j of distinct points with smallest Euclidean distance between them.

```
// base case of <= 3 points omitted
```
1 L_x := first half of P_x, sorted by x-coordinate
2 L_y := first half of P_x, sorted by y-coordinate
3 R_x := second half of P_x, sorted by x-coordinate
4 R_y := second half of P_x, sorted by y-coordinate

5 $(l_1, l_2) := $ ClosestPair(L_x, L_y) // best left pair
6 $(r_1, r_2) := $ ClosestPair(R_x, R_y) // best right pair
7 $(s_1, s_2) := $ ClosestSplitPair(P_x, P_y) // best split pair

8 return best of (l_1, l_2), (r_1, r_2), (s_1, s_2)

In the omitted base case, when there are two or three input points, the algorithm computes the closest pair directly in constant ($O(1)$) time. Deriving L_x and R_x from P_x is easy (just split P_x in half). To compute L_y and R_y, the algorithm can perform a linear scan over P_y, putting each point at the end of either L_y or R_y, according to the point's x-coordinate. We conclude that lines 1–4 can be implemented in $O(n)$ time.

Provided we implement the ClosestSplitPair subroutine correctly, the algorithm is guaranteed to compute the closest pair of points—the three subroutine calls in lines 5–7 cover all possibilities for where the closest pair might be.

Quiz 3.4

Suppose that we correctly implement the ClosestSplitPair subroutine in $O(n)$ time. What will be the overall running time of the ClosestPair algorithm? (Choose the smallest upper bound that applies.)

a) $O(n)$

b) $O(n \log n)$

c) $O(n(\log n)^2)$

d) $O(n^2)$

(See Section 3.4.10 for the solution and discussion.)

3.4.5   A Subtle Tweak

The solution to Quiz 3.4 makes our goal clear: we want an $O(n)$-time implementation of the ClosestSplitPair subroutine, leading to an overall running time bound of $O(n \log n)$ and matching the running time of our algorithm for the one-dimensional special case.

We'll design a slightly weaker subroutine that is adequate for our purposes. Here's the key observation: *we need the ClosestSplitPair subroutine to identify the closest split pair only when it is the closest pair overall.* If the closest pair is a left or right pair, ClosestSplitPair might as well return garbage—line 8 of the pseudocode in Section 3.4.4 will ignore its suggested point pair anyway, in favor of the actual closest pair computed by one of the recursive calls. Our algorithm will make crucial use of this relaxed correctness requirement.

To implement this idea, we'll explicitly pass to the ClosestSplitPair subroutine the distance δ between the closest pair that is a left or right pair; the subroutine then knows that it has to worry only about split pairs with interpoint distance less than δ. In other words, we replace lines 7–8 of the pseudocode in Section 3.4.4 with the following.

ClosestPair (**Addendum**)

7 $\delta := \min\{d(l_1, l_2), d(r_1, r_2)\}$
8 $(s_1, s_2) := \text{ClosestSplitPair}(P_x, P_y, \delta)$
9 return best of $(l_1, l_2), (r_1, r_2), (s_1, s_2)$

3.4.6 `ClosestSplitPair`

We now provide an implementation of the `ClosestSplitPair` subroutine that runs in linear time and correctly computes the closest pair whenever it is a split pair. You may not believe that the following pseudocode satisfies these requirements, but it does. The high-level idea is to do brute-force search over a cleverly restricted set of point pairs.

`ClosestSplitPair`

Input: two copies P_x and P_y of $n \geq 2$ points in the plane, sorted by x- and y-coordinate, and a parameter δ.

Output: the closest pair, provided it is a split pair.

---

1 $\bar{x} :=$ largest x-coordinate in left half   `// median`
    `x-coordinate`
2 $S_y :=$ {points $q_1, q_2, \ldots, q_\ell$ with x-coordinate
          between $\bar{x} - \delta$ and $\bar{x} + \delta$, sorted by y-coordinate}
3 $best := \delta$
4 $bestPair := NULL$
5 **for** $i := 1$ **to** $\ell - 1$ **do**
6   **for** $j := 1$ **to** $\min\{7, \ell - i\}$ **do**
7   **if** $d(q_i, q_{i+j}) < best$ **then**
8              $best := d(q_i, q_{i+j})$
9              $bestPair := (q_i, q_{i+j})$
10 return $bestPair$

The subroutine begins in line 1 by identifying the rightmost point in the left half of the point set, which defines the "median x-coordinate" $\bar{x}$. A pair of points is a split pair if and only if one point has x-coordinate at most $\bar{x}$ and the other greater than $\bar{x}$. Computing $\bar{x}$ takes constant $(O(1))$ time because P_x stores the points sorted by x-coordinate (the median is the $\frac{n}{2}$th array entry). In line 2 the subroutine performs a filtering step, discarding all points except those lying in the vertical strip of width 2δ centered at $\bar{x}$ (Figure 3.5). The set S_y can be computed in linear time by scanning through P_y and removing any points with an x-coordinate outside the range of interest.[13] Lines 5–9 perform brute-force search over the pairs of points of S_y that have at most 6 points in between them (in the ordering of S_y by y-coordinates), and computes the closest such pair of points.[14] You can think of this as an extension of our algorithm for the one-dimensional case, in which we examine all "nearly consecutive" pairs of points. The total number of loop iterations is less than $7\ell \leq 7n = O(n)$, and the algorithm performs a constant number of primitive operations in each iteration. We conclude that the ClosestSplitPair subroutine runs in $O(n)$ time, as desired. But why on Earth should it ever find the closest pair?

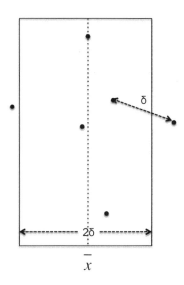

Figure 3.5: The ClosestSplitPair subroutine. S_y is the set of points enclosed by the vertical strip. δ is the smallest distance between a left pair or a right pair of points. The split point pairs have one point on either side of the dotted line.

---

[13]This step is the reason why we sorted the point set by y-coordinate once and for all in the initial preprocessing step. Since we're shooting for a linear-time subroutine, there's no time to sort them now!

[14]If there is no such pair of points at distance less than δ, then the subroutine returns NULL. In this case, in ClosestPair, this NULL pair is ignored and the final comparison is between only the point pairs returned by the two recursive calls.

3.4.7   Correctness

The `ClosestSplitPair` subroutine runs in linear time because, out of the quadratic number of possible point pairs, it searches over only a linear number of them. How do we know it didn't miss out on the true closest pair? The following lemma, which is a bit shocking, guarantees that when the closest pair is a split pair, its points appear nearly consecutively in the filtered set S_y.

Lemma 3.3 *In the* `ClosestSplitPair` *subroutine, suppose (p, q) is a split pair with $d(p, q) < \delta$, where δ is the smallest distance between a left pair or right pair of points. Then:*

(a) p and q will be included in the set S_y;

(b) at most six points of S_y have a y-coordinate in between those of p and q.

This lemma is far from obvious, and we prove it in the next section.

Lemma 3.3 implies that the `ClosestSplitPair` subroutine does its job.

Corollary 3.4 *When the closest pair is a split pair, the* `ClosestSplitPair` *subroutine returns it.*

Proof: Assume that the closest pair (p, q) is a split pair, and so $d(p, q) < \delta$, where δ is the minimum distance between a left or right pair. Then, Lemma 3.3 ensures that both p and q belong to the set S_y in the `ClosestSplitPair` subroutine, and that there are at most six points of S_y between them in y-coordinate. Since `ClosestSplitPair` exhaustively searches over all pairs of points that satisfy these two properties, it will compute the closest such pair, which must be the actual closest pair (p, q). *QED*

Pending the proof of Lemma 3.3, we now have a correct and blazingly fast algorithm for the closest pair problem.

Theorem 3.5 (Computing the Closest Pair) *For every set P of $n \geq 2$ points in the plane, the* `ClosestPair` *algorithm correctly computes the closest pair of P and runs in $O(n \log n)$ time.*

Proof: We have already argued the running time bound: the algorithm spends $O(n \log n)$ time in its preprocessing step, and the rest of the algorithm has the same asymptotic running time as `MergeSort` (with two recursive calls each on half the input, plus linear additional work), which is also $O(n \log n)$.

For correctness, if the closest pair is a left pair, it is returned by the first recursive call (line 5 in Section 3.4.4); if it is a right pair, it is returned by the second recursive call (line 6). If it is a split pair, then Corollary 3.4 guarantees that it is returned by the `ClosestSplitPair` subroutine. In all cases, the closest pair is among the three candidates examined by the algorithm (line 9 in Section 3.4.5), and will be returned as the final answer. $\mathcal{QED}$

3.4.8   Proof of Lemma 3.3(a)

Part (a) of Lemma 3.3 is the easier part. Assume that there is a split pair (p, q), with p in the left half of the point set and q in the right half, such that $d(p, q) < \delta$, where δ is the minimum distance between a left or right pair. Write $p = (x_1, y_1)$ and $q = (x_2, y_2)$, and let $\bar{x}$ denote the x-coordinate of the rightmost point of the left half. Since p and q are in the left and right halves, respectively, we have

$$x_1 \leq \bar{x} < x_2.$$

At the same time, x_1 and x_2 cannot be very different. Formally, remembering the definition of Euclidean distance (3.5), we can write

$$\begin{aligned}
\delta &> d(p, q) \\
&= \sqrt{(x_1 - x_2)^2 + (y_1 - y_2)^2} \\
&\geq \sqrt{\max\{(x_1 - x_2)^2, (y_1 - y_2)^2\}} \\
&= \max\{|x_1 - x_2|, |y_1 - y_2|\}.
\end{aligned}$$

This means that p and q differ by less than δ in both their x- and y-coordinates:

$$|x_1 - x_2|, |y_1 - y_2| < \delta. \tag{3.6}$$

Since $x_1 \leq \bar{x}$ and x_2 is at most δ larger than x_1, we have $x_2 \leq \bar{x} + \delta$.[15] Since $x_2 \geq \bar{x}$ and x_1 is at most δ smaller than x_2, $x_1 \geq \bar{x} - \delta$.

---

[15]Imagine that p and q are people tied at the waist by a rope of length δ. The point p can travel only as far rightward as $\bar{x}$, which limits q's travels to $\bar{x} + \delta$ (Figure 3.6).

In particular, p and q both have x-coordinates that are wedged in between $\bar{x} - \delta$ and $\bar{x} + \delta$. All such points, including p and q, belong to the set S_y.

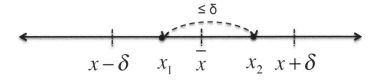

Figure 3.6: Proof of Lemma 3.3(a). Both p and q have x-coordinates between $\bar{x} - \delta$ and $\bar{x} + \delta$.

3.4.9   Proof of Lemma 3.3(b)

Recall our standing assumptions: there is a split pair (p, q), with $p = (x_1, y_1)$ in the left half of the point set and $q = (x_2, y_2)$ in the right half, such that $d(p, q) < \delta$, where δ is the minimum distance between a left or right pair. Lemma 3.3(b) asserts that p and q not only appear in the set S_y (as proved in part (a)), but that they are nearly consecutive, with at most six other points of S_y possessing y-coordinates between y_1 and y_2.

For the proof, we draw eight boxes in the plane in a 2×4 pattern, where each box has side length $\frac{\delta}{2}$ (Figure 3.7). There are two columns of boxes on either side of $\bar{x}$, the median x-coordinate. The bottom of the boxes is aligned with the lower of the points p and q, at the y-coordinate $\min\{y_1, y_2\}$.[16]

From part (a), we know that both p and q have x-coordinates between $\bar{x} - \delta$ and $\bar{x} + \delta$. For concreteness, suppose q has the smaller y-coordinate; the other case is analogous. Thus, q appears at the bottom of some box on the bottom row (in the right half). Since p's y-coordinate can only be δ larger than q's (see (3.6)), p also appears in one of the boxes (in the left half). Every point of S_y with y-coordinate between p and q has x-coordinate between $\bar{x} - \delta$ and $\bar{x} + \delta$

---

[16]Don't forget: these boxes are purely for the sake of reasoning about why the `ClosestPair` algorithm is correct. The algorithm itself knows nothing about these boxes, and remains just the pseudocode in Sections 3.4.4–3.4.6.

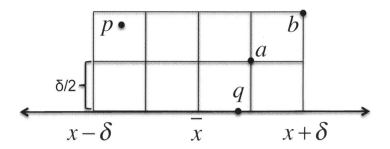

Figure 3.7: Proof of Lemma 3.3(b). The points p and q inhabit two of these eight boxes, and there is at most one point in each box.

(the requirement for membership in S_y) and y-coordinate between y_2 and $y_1 < y_2 + \delta$, and hence lies in one of the eight boxes.

The worry is that there are lots of points in these boxes that have y-coordinate between y_1 and y_2. To show that this can't happen, let's prove that each box contains at most one point. Then, the eight boxes contain at most eight points (including p and q), and there can only be six points of S_y in between p and q in y-coordinate.[17]

Why does each box have at most one point? This is the part of the argument that uses our observation in Section 3.4.5 and the fact that δ is the smallest distance between a left pair or a right pair. To derive a contradiction, suppose that some box has two points, a and b (one of which might be p or q). This point pair is either a left pair (if the points are in the first two columns) or a right pair (if they are in the last two). The farthest apart that a and b can be is at opposite corners of the box (Figure 3.7), in which case, by the Pythagorean theorem[18], the distance between a and b is $\sqrt{2} \cdot \frac{\delta}{2} < \delta$. But this contradicts the assumption that there is no left or right pair at a distance less than δ! This contradiction implies that each of the eight boxes in Figure 3.7 has at most one point; hence, at most six points of S_y have a y-coordinate between those of p and q. $\mathcal{QED}$

---

[17]If a point has x-coordinate exactly $\bar{x}$, count it toward the box to its left. Other points on the boundary of multiple boxes can be assigned arbitrarily to one of them.

[18]For a right triangle, the sum of the squares of the sides equals the square of the hypotenuse.

3.4.10   Solution to Quiz 3.4

Correct answer: (b). The correct answer is $O(n \log n)$. $O(n)$ is not correct because, among other reasons, the ClosestPair algorithm already spends $\Theta(n \log n)$ time in its preprocessing step creating the sorted lists P_x and P_y. The upper bound of $O(n \log n)$ follows from the exact same argument as for MergeSort: the ClosestPair algorithm makes two recursive calls, each on an input of half the size, and performs $O(n)$ work outside its recursive calls. (Recall that lines 1–4 and 8 can be implemented in $O(n)$ time, and for this quiz we are assuming that ClosestSplitPair also runs in linear time.) This pattern perfectly matches the one we already analyzed for MergeSort in Section 1.5, so we know that the total number of operations performed is $O(n \log n)$. Since the preprocessing step also runs in $O(n \log n)$ time, the final running time bound is $O(n \log n)$.

The Upshot

★ A divide-and-conquer algorithm divides the input into smaller subproblems, conquers the subproblems recursively, and combines the subproblem solutions into a solution for the original problem.

★ Computing the number of inversions in an array is relevant for measuring similarity between two ranked lists. The brute-force search algorithm for the problem runs in $\Theta(n^2)$ time for arrays of length n.

★ There is a divide-and-conquer algorithm that piggybacks on MergeSort and computes the number of inversions in $O(n \log n)$ time.

★ Strassen's subcubic-time divide-and-conquer algorithm for matrix multiplication is a mind-blowing example of how algorithmic ingenuity can improve over straightforward solutions. The key idea is to save a recursive call over a sim-

pler divide-and-conquer algorithm, analogous
to Karatsuba multiplication.

★ In the closest pair problem, the input is n points
  in the plane, and the goal is to compute the
  pair of points with smallest Euclidean distance
  between them. The brute-force search algorithm
  runs in $\Theta(n^2)$ time.

★ There is a sophisticated divide-and-conquer algorithm that solves the closest pair problem in
  $O(n \log n)$ time.

Test Your Understanding

Problem 3.1 Consider the following pseudocode for calculating a^b,
where a and b are positive integers:[19]

FastPower

Input: positive integers a and b.
Output: a^b.

---

if $b = 1$ **then**
    return a
else
    $c := a \cdot a$
    $ans := \texttt{FastPower}(c, \lfloor b/2 \rfloor)$
if b is odd **then**
    return $a \cdot ans$
else
    return ans

Assume for this problem that each multiplication and division can be
performed in constant time. What is the asymptotic running time of
this algorithm, as a function of b?

---

[19]The notation $\lfloor x \rfloor$ denotes the "floor" function, which rounds its argument
down to the nearest integer.

a) $\Theta(\log b)$

b) $\Theta(\sqrt{b})$

c) $\Theta(b)$

d) $\Theta(b \log b)$

Challenge Problems

Problem 3.2 *(S)* You are given a *unimodal* array of n distinct elements, meaning that its entries are in increasing order up until its maximum element, after which its elements are in decreasing order. Give an algorithm to compute the maximum element of a unimodal array that runs in $O(\log n)$ time.

Problem 3.3 *(S)* You are given a sorted (from smallest to largest) array A of n distinct integers which can be positive, negative, or zero. Design the fastest algorithm you can for deciding whether or not there is an index i such that $A[i] = i$.

Problem 3.4 (Difficult.) You are given an n-by-n grid of distinct numbers. A number is a *local minimum* if it is smaller than all its neighbors. (A *neighbor* of a number is one immediately above, below, to the left, or to the right. Most numbers have four neighbors; numbers on the side have three; the four corners have two.) Use the divide-and-conquer algorithm design paradigm to compute a local minimum with only $O(n)$ comparisons between pairs of numbers. (Note: since there are n^2 numbers in the input, you cannot afford to look at all of them.)

[Hint: Figure out how to recurse on an $\frac{n}{2}$-by-$\frac{n}{2}$ grid after doing only $O(n)$ work.]

Programming Problems

Problem 3.5 Implement in your favorite programming language the CountInv algorithm from Section 3.2 for counting the number of inversions of an array. (See www.algorithmsilluminated.org for test cases and challenge data sets.)

Chapter 4

The Master Method

This chapter presents a "black-box" method for determining the running time of recursive algorithms—plug in a few key characteristics of the algorithm, and out pops an upper bound on the algorithm's running time. This "master method" applies to most of the divide-and-conquer algorithms you'll ever see, including Karatsuba's integer multiplication algorithm (Section 1.3) and Strassen's matrix multiplication algorithm (Section 3.3).[1] This chapter also illustrates a more general theme in the study of algorithms: properly evaluating novel algorithmic ideas often requires non-obvious mathematical analysis.

After introducing recurrences in Section 4.1, we give a formal statement of the master method (Section 4.2) and look at six example applications (Section 4.3). Section 4.4 covers the proof of the master method, with an emphasis on the meaning behind its famous three cases. The proof builds nicely on our analysis of the MergeSort algorithm in Section 1.5.

4.1   Integer Multiplication Revisited

To motivate the master method, let's recall the main points of our integer multiplication discussion (Sections 1.2–1.3). The problem is to multiply two n-digit numbers, where the primitive operations are the addition or multiplication of two single-digit numbers. The iterative grade-school algorithm requires $\Theta(n^2)$ operations to multiply two n-digit numbers. Can we do better with a divide-and-conquer approach?

---

[1]The master method is also called the "master theorem."

4.1.1   The `RecIntMult` Algorithm

The `RecIntMult` algorithm from Section 1.3 creates smaller subproblems by breaking the given n-digit numbers x and y into their first and second halves: $x = 10^{n/2} \cdot a + b$ and $y = 10^{n/2} \cdot c + d$, where a, b, c, d are $n/2$-digit numbers (assuming n is even, for simplicity). For example, if $x = 1234$, then $a = 12$ and $b = 34$. Then

$$x \cdot y = 10^n \cdot (a \cdot c) + 10^{n/2} \cdot (a \cdot d + b \cdot c) + b \cdot d, \qquad (4.1)$$

which shows that multiplying two n-digit numbers reduces to multiplying four pairs of $n/2$-digit numbers, plus $O(n)$ additional work (for appending zeroes appropriately and grade-school addition).

   The way to describe this formally is by a *recurrence*. Let $T(n)$ denote the maximum number of operations used by this recursive algorithm to multiply two n-digit numbers—this is the quantity we want to bound from above. A recurrence expresses a running time bound $T(n)$ in terms of the number of operations performed by recursive calls. The recurrence for the `RecIntMult` algorithm is

$$T(n) \leq \underbrace{4 \cdot T\left(\frac{n}{2}\right)}_{\text{work done by recursive calls}} + \underbrace{O(n)}_{\text{work done outside recursive calls}}.$$

Like a recursive algorithm, a recurrence also needs a base case, which states what $T(n)$ is for values of n that are too small to trigger any recursive calls. Here, the base case is when $n = 1$, and the algorithm just performs a single multiplication, so $T(1) = 1$.

4.1.2   The `Karatsuba` Algorithm

Karatsuba's recursive algorithm for integer multiplication uses a trick due to Gauss to save one recursive call. The trick is to recursively compute the products of a and c, b and d, and $a + b$ and $c + d$, and extract the middle coefficient $a \cdot d + b \cdot c$ via $(a + b)(c + d) - ac - bd$. This is enough information to compute the right-hand side of (4.1) with $O(n)$ additional primitive operations.

Quiz 4.1

Which recurrence best describes the running time of the `Karatsuba` algorithm for integer multiplication?

a) $T(n) \leq 2 \cdot T\left(\frac{n}{2}\right) + O(n^2)$

b) $3 \cdot T\left(\frac{n}{2}\right) + O(n)$

c) $3 \cdot T\left(\frac{n}{2}\right) + O(n^2)$

d) $4 \cdot T\left(\frac{n}{2}\right) + O(n)$

(See below for the solution and discussion.)

Correct answer: (b). The only change from the `RecIntMult` algorithm is that the number of recursive calls has dropped by one. It's true that the amount of work done outside the recursive calls is larger in the `Karatsuba` algorithm, but only by a constant factor that gets suppressed in the big-O notation. The appropriate recurrence for the `Karatsuba` algorithm is therefore

$$T(n) \leq \underbrace{3 \cdot T\left(\frac{n}{2}\right)}_{\text{work done by recursive calls}} + \underbrace{O(n)}_{\text{work done outside recursive calls}},$$

again with the base case $T(1) = 1$.[2]

4.1.3 Comparing the Recurrences

At the moment, we don't know the running time of `RecIntMult` or `Karatsuba`, but inspecting their recurrences suggests that the latter can only be faster than the former. Another point of comparison is the `MergeSort` algorithm, where our analysis in Section 1.5 leads to the recurrence

$$T(n) \leq \underbrace{2 \cdot T\left(\frac{n}{2}\right)}_{\text{work done by recursive calls}} + \underbrace{O(n)}_{\text{work done outside recursive calls}},$$

where n is the length of the array to be sorted. This suggests that our running time bounds for both the `RecIntMult` and `Karatsuba` algorithms cannot be better than our bound for `MergeSort`, which is $O(n \log n)$. Beyond these clues, we really have no idea what the running time of either algorithm is. Enlightenment awaits with the master method, discussed next.

---

[2]Technically, the recursive call on $a + b$ and $c + d$ might involve $(\frac{n}{2} + 1)$-digit numbers. Among friends, let's ignore this—it doesn't matter in the final analysis.

4.2   Formal Statement

The master method is exactly what you'd want for analyzing recursive algorithms. It takes as input the recurrence for the algorithm and—boom—spits out as output an upper bound on the running time of the algorithm.

4.2.1   Standard Recurrences

We'll discuss a version of the master method that handles what we'll call "standard recurrences," which have three free parameters and the following form.[3]

Standard Recurrence Format

Base case: $T(n)$ is at most a constant for all sufficiently small n.[4]

General case: for larger values of n,

$$T(n) \leq a \cdot T\left(\frac{n}{b}\right) + O(n^d).$$

Parameters:

- a = number of recursive calls

- b = input size shrinkage factor

- d = exponent in running time of the "combine step"

The base case of a standard recurrence asserts that once the input size is so small that no recursive calls are needed, the problem can be solved in $O(1)$ time. This will be the case for all the applications we consider. The general case assumes that the algorithm makes a recursive calls, each on a subproblem with size a b factor smaller than its input, and does $O(n^d)$ work outside these recursive calls. For

---

[3]This presentation of the master method draws inspiration from Chapter 2 of *Algorithms*, by Sanjoy Dasgupta, Christos Papadimitriou, and Umesh Vazirani (McGraw-Hill, 2006).

[4]Formally, there exist positive integers n_0 and c, independent of n, such that $T(n) \leq c$ for all $n \leq n_0$.

example, in the `MergeSort` algorithm, there are two recursive calls
($a = 2$), each on an array of half the size of the input ($b = 2$), and
$O(n)$ work is done outside the recursive calls ($d = 1$). In general, a
can be any positive integer, b can be any real number bigger than 1
(if $b \leq 1$ then the algorithm won't terminate), and d can be any
nonnegative real number, with $d = 0$ indicating only constant ($O(1)$)
work beyond the recursive calls. As usual, we ignore the detail that
$\frac{n}{b}$ might need to be rounded up or down to an integer—and as usual,
it doesn't affect our final conclusions. Never forget that a, b, and
d should be *constants*—numbers that are independent of the input
size n.[5] Typical values for these parameters are 1 (for a and d), 2,
3, and 4. If you ever find yourself saying something like "apply the
master method with $a = n$ or $b = \frac{n}{n-1}$," you're using it incorrectly.

One restriction in standard recurrences is that every recursive
call is on a subproblem of the same size. For example, an algorithm
that recurses once on the first third of an input array and once on
the rest would lead to a non-standard recurrence. Most (but not all)
natural divide-and-conquer algorithms lead to standard recurrences.
For example, in the `MergeSort` algorithm, both recursive calls operate
on problems with size half that of the input array. In our recursive
integer multiplication algorithms, recursive calls are always given
numbers with half as many digits.[6]

4.2.2 Statement and Discussion of the Master Method

We can now state the master method, which provides an upper bound
on a standard recurrence as a function of the key parameters a, b,
and d.

Theorem 4.1 (Master Method) *If $T(n)$ is defined by a standard
recurrence, with parameters $a \geq 1$, $b > 1$, and $d \geq 0$, then*

$$T(n) = \begin{cases} O(n^d \log n) & \text{if } a = b^d & \text{[Case 1]} \\ O(n^d) & \text{if } a < b^d & \text{[Case 2]} \\ O(n^{\log_b a}) & \text{if } a > b^d & \text{[Case 3].} \end{cases} \qquad (4.2)$$

---

[5]There are also the constants suppressed in the base case and in the "$O(n^d)$"
term, but the conclusion of the master method does not depend on their values.

[6]There are more general versions of the master method that accommodate a
wider family of recurrences, but the simple version here is sufficient for almost
any divide-and-conquer algorithm you're likely to encounter.

What's up with the three cases, and why are the relative values of a and b^d so important? In the second case, could the running time of the whole algorithm really be only $O(n^d)$, when the outermost recursive call already does $O(n^d)$ work? And what's the deal with the exotic-looking running time bound in the third case? By the end of this chapter we'll learn satisfying answers to all of these questions, and the statement of the master method will seem like the most natural thing in the world.[7]

More On Logarithms

Another puzzling aspect of Theorem 4.1 concerns the inconsistent use of logarithms. The third case carefully states that the logarithm in question is base-b—the number of times you can divide n by b before the result is at most 1. Meanwhile, the first case does not specify the base of the logarithm at all. The reason is that *any two logarithmic functions differ only by a constant factor.* For example, the base-2 logarithm always exceeds the natural logarithm (i.e., the base-e logarithm, where $e = 2.718\ldots$) by a factor of $1/\ln 2 \approx 1.44$. In the first case of the master method, changing the base of the logarithm only changes the constant factor that is conveniently suppressed in the big-O notation. In the third case, the logarithm appears in the exponent, where different constant factors translate to very different running time bounds (like n^2 vs. n^{100})!

4.3   Six Examples

The master method (Theorem 4.1) is hard to get your head around the first time you see it. Let's instantiate it in six different examples.

---

[7]The bounds in Theorem 4.1 have the form $O(f(n))$ rather than $\Theta(f(n))$ because in our recurrence we only assume an upper bound on $T(n)$. If we replace "$\leq$" with "$=$" and $O(n^d)$ with $\Theta(n^d)$ in the definition of a standard recurrence, the bounds in Theorem 4.1 hold with $O(\cdot)$ replaced by $\Theta(\cdot)$. Verifying this is a good way to check your understanding of the proof in Section 4.4.

4.3.1   `MergeSort` **Revisited**

As a sanity check, let's revisit an algorithm whose running time we already know, `MergeSort`. To apply the master method, all we need to do is identify the values of the three free parameters: a, the number of recursive calls; b, the factor by which the input size shrinks prior to the recursive calls; and d, the exponent in the bound on the amount of work done outside the recursive calls.[8] In `MergeSort`, there are two recursive calls, so $a = 2$. Each recursive call receives half of the input array, so $b = 2$ as well. The work done outside these recursive calls is dominated by the `Merge` subroutine, which runs in linear time (Section 1.5.1), and so $d = 1$. Thus

$$a = 2 = 2^1 = b^d,$$

putting us in the first case of the master method. Plugging in the parameters, Theorem 4.1 tells us that the running time of `MergeSort` is $O(n^d \log n) = O(n \log n)$, thereby replicating our analysis in Section 1.5.

4.3.2   **Binary Search**

For our second example, we consider the problem of searching a sorted array for a given element. Think, for example, of searching for your own name in an alphabetical list in a large book.[9] You could search linearly starting from the beginning, but this would squander the advantage that the list is in alphabetical order. A smarter approach is to look in the middle of the book and recurse on either its first half (if the name in the middle comes after your own) or its second half (otherwise). This algorithm, translated to the problem of searching a sorted array, is known as *binary search*.[10]

What's the running time of binary search? This question is easy to answer directly, but let's see how the master method handles it.

---

[8] All of the recurrences we consider have a base case in the form required for standard recurrences, and we won't discuss them from here on out.

[9] Readers of at least a certain age should be reminded of a phone book.

[10] If you haven't walked through the code of this algorithm before, look it up in your favorite introductory programming book or tutorial.

Quiz 4.2

What are the respective values of a, b, and d for the binary search algorithm?

   a) $1, 2, 0$ [case 1]

   b) $1, 2, 1$ [case 2]

   c) $2, 2, 0$ [case 3]

   d) $2, 2, 1$ [case 1]

(See Section 4.3.7 for the solution and discussion.)

4.3.3   Recursive Integer Multiplication

Now we get to the good stuff, divide-and-conquer algorithms for which we don't yet know a running time bound. Let's begin with the RecIntMult algorithm for integer multiplication. We saw in Section 4.1 that the appropriate recurrence for this algorithm is

$$T(n) \leq 4 \cdot T\left(\frac{n}{2}\right) + O(n),$$

and so $a = 4$, $b = 2$, and $d = 1$. Thus

$$a = 4 > 2 = 2^1 = b^d,$$

putting us in the third case of the master method. In this case, we obtain the exotic-looking running time bound of $O(n^{\log_b a})$. For our parameter values, this is $O(n^{\log_2 4}) = O(n^2)$. Thus the RecIntMult algorithm matches but does not outperform the iterative grade-school algorithm for integer multiplication (which uses $\Theta(n^2)$ operations).

4.3.4   Karatsuba Multiplication

A divide-and-conquer approach to integer multiplication pays off only once Gauss's trick is used to save a recursive call. As we saw in Section 4.1, the running time of the Karatsuba algorithm is governed by the recurrence

$$T(n) \leq 3 \cdot T\left(\frac{n}{2}\right) + O(n),$$

which differs from the previous recurrence only in that a has dropped from 4 to 3 (b is still 2, d is still 1). We expect the running time to be somewhere between $O(n \log n)$ (the bound when $a = 2$, as in MergeSort) and $O(n^2)$ (the bound when $a = 4$, as in RecIntMult). If the suspense is killing you, the master method offers a quick resolution: we have

$$a = 3 > 2 = 2^1 = b^d,$$

and so we are still in the third case of the master method, but with an improved running time bound: $O(n^{\log_b a}) = O(n^{\log_2 3}) = O(n^{1.59})$. Thus saving a recursive call leads to a fundamentally better running time, and the integer multiplication algorithm that you learned in the third grade is not the fastest possible![11]

4.3.5 Matrix Multiplication

Section 3.3 considered the problem of multiplying two $n \times n$ matrices. As with integer multiplication, we discussed three algorithms—a straightforward iterative algorithm, the straightforward recursive RecMatMult algorithm, and the ingenious Strassen algorithm. The iterative algorithm uses $\Theta(n^3)$ operations (Quiz 3.3). The RecMatMult algorithm breaks each of the two input matrices into four $\frac{n}{2} \times \frac{n}{2}$ matrices (one for each quadrant), performs the corresponding eight recursive calls on smaller matrices, and combines the results appropriately (using straightforward matrix addition). The Strassen algorithm cleverly identifies seven pairs of $\frac{n}{2} \times \frac{n}{2}$ matrices whose products suffice to reconstruct the product of the original input matrices.

Quiz 4.3

What running time bounds does the master method provide for the RecMatMult and Strassen algorithms, respectively?

a) $O(n^3)$ and $O(n^2)$

b) $O(n^3)$ and $O(n^{\log_2 7})$

---

[11]Fun fact: in the Python programming language, the built-in subroutine for multiplying integer objects uses the grade-school algorithm for integers with at most 70 digits, and the Karatsuba algorithm otherwise.

c) $O(n^3)$ and $O(n^3)$

d) $O(n^3 \log n)$ and $O(n^3)$

(See Section 4.3.7 for the solution and discussion.)

4.3.6   A Fictitious Recurrence

In our five examples thus far, two recurrences have fallen in the first case of the master method, and the rest in the third case. There are also naturally occurring recurrences that fall in the second case. For example, suppose we have a divide-and-conquer algorithm that operates like MergeSort, except that the algorithm works harder outside the recursive calls, doing a quadratic rather than linear amount of work. That is, consider the recurrence

$$T(n) \le 2 \cdot T\left(\frac{n}{2}\right) + O(n^2).$$

Here, we have

$$a = 2 < 4 = 2^2 = b^d,$$

putting us squarely in the second case of the master method, for a running time bound of $O(n^d) = O(n^2)$. This might seem counterintuitive; given that the MergeSort algorithm does linear work outside the two recursive calls and has a running time of $O(n \log n)$, you might expect that a quadratic-time combine step would lead to a running time of $O(n^2 \log n)$. The master method shows this to be an overestimate, and provides the better upper bound of $O(n^2)$. Remarkably, this means that the total running time of the algorithm is dominated by the work done in the outermost call—all subsequent recursive calls only increase the total number of operations performed by a constant factor.[12]

4.3.7   Solutions to Quizzes 4.2–4.3

Solution to Quiz 4.2

Correct answer: (a). Binary search recurses on either the left half of the input array or the right half (never both), so there is only one

---

[12]We'll see another example of case 2 of the master method when we discuss linear-time selection in Chapter 6.

recursive call ($a = 1$). This recursive call is on half of the input array, so b is again equal to 2. Outside the recursive call, all binary search does is a single comparison (between the middle element of the array and the element being searched for) to determine whether to recurse on the left or the right half of the array. This translates to $O(1)$ work outside the recursive call, so $d = 0$. Since $a = 1 = 2^0 = b^d$, we are again in the first case of the master method, and we get a running time bound of $O(n^d \log n) = O(\log n)$.

Solution to Quiz 4.3

Correct answer: (b). Let's start with the `RecMatMult` algorithm (Section 3.3.4). Let $T(n)$ denote the maximum number of primitive operations that the algorithm uses to multiply two $n \times n$ matrices. The number a of recursive calls is 8. Each of these calls is on a pair of $\frac{n}{2} \times \frac{n}{2}$ matrices, so $b = 2$. The work done outside the recursive calls involves a constant number of matrix additions, and these require $O(n^2)$ time (constant time for each of the n^2 matrix entries). Thus the recurrence is

$$T(n) \le 8 \cdot T\left(\frac{n}{2}\right) + O(n^2),$$

and since

$$a = 8 > 4 = 2^2 = b^d,$$

we are in the third case of the master method, which gives a running time bound of $O(n^{\log_b a}) = O(n^{\log_2 8}) = O(n^3)$.

The only difference between the recurrence for the `Strassen` algorithm and the recurrence above is that the number a of recursive calls drops from 8 to 7. It's true that the `Strassen` algorithm does more matrix additions than `RecMatMult`, but only by a constant factor, and hence d is still equal to 2. Thus

$$a = 7 > 4 = 2^2 = b^d.$$

We are still in the third case of the master method, but with an improved running time bound: $O(n^{\log_b a}) = O(n^{\log_2 7}) = O(n^{2.81})$. Thus the `Strassen` algorithm really is asymptotically superior to the straightforward iterative algorithm![13]

*4.4   Proof of the Master Method

This section proves the master method (Theorem 4.1): if $T(n)$ is governed by a standard recurrence, of the form

$$T(n) \leq a \cdot T\left(\frac{n}{b}\right) + O(n^d),$$

then

$$T(n) = \begin{cases} O(n^d \log n) & \text{if } a = b^d \quad \text{[Case 1]} \\ O(n^d) & \text{if } a < b^d \quad \text{[Case 2]} \\ O(n^{\log_b a}) & \text{if } a > b^d \quad \text{[Case 3]}. \end{cases}$$

It's important to remember the meanings of the three free parameters:

Parameter	Meaning
a	number of recursive calls
b	factor by which input size shrinks in recursive call
d	exponent of work done outside recursive calls

4.4.1   Preamble

The proof of the master method is important not because we care about formality for its own sake, but because it provides the fundamental explanation for why things are the way they are—for example, why the master method has three cases. With this in mind, you should distinguish between two types of content in the proof. At a couple points we will resort to algebraic computations to understand what's going on. These calculations are worth seeing once in your life, but they are not particularly important to remember in the long term. What is worth remembering is the conceptual meaning of the three cases of the master method. The proof will use the recursion tree approach that served us so well for analyzing the MergeSort algorithm (Section 1.5), and the three cases correspond to three different types

---

[13]There is a long line of research papers that devise increasingly sophisticated matrix multiplication algorithms with ever-better worst-case asymptotic running times (albeit with large constant factors that preclude practical implementations). The current world record is a running time bound of roughly $O(n^{2.3729})$, and for all we know there could be an $O(n^2)$-time algorithm waiting to be discovered.

of recursion trees. If you can remember the meaning of the three cases, there is no need to memorize the running times in the master method—you will be able to reverse engineer them as needed from your conceptual understanding of it.

For the formal proof, we should explicitly write out all the constant factors in the recurrence:

Base case: $T(1) \leq c.$

General case: for $n > 1$,

$$T(n) \leq a \cdot T\left(\frac{n}{b}\right) + cn^d. \qquad (4.3)$$

For simplicity we're assuming that the constant n_0 specifying when the base case kicks in is 1; the proof for a different constant n_0 is pretty much the same. We can assume that the suppressed constants in the base case and the $O(n^d)$ term in the general case are equal to the same number c; if they were different constants, we could just work with the larger of the two. Finally, let's focus on the case in which n is a power of b. The proof for the general case is similar, with no additional conceptual content, but is more tedious.

4.4.2   Recursion Trees Revisited

The high-level plan for the proof is as natural as could be: generalize the recursion tree argument for MergeSort (Section 1.5) so that it accommodates other values of the key parameters a, b, and d. Recall that a recursion tree provides a principled way to keep track of all the work done by a recursive algorithm, across all its recursive calls. Nodes of the tree correspond to recursive calls, and the children of a node correspond to the recursive calls made by that node (Figure 4.1). Thus the root (level 0) of the recursion tree corresponds to the outermost call to the algorithm, level 1 has a nodes corresponding to its recursive calls, and so on. The leaves at the bottom of the tree correspond to recursive calls where the base case is triggered.

As in our analysis of MergeSort, we'd like to account level-by-level for the work performed by a recursive algorithm. This plan requires understanding two things: the number of distinct subproblems at a given recursion level j, and the length of the input to each of these subproblems.

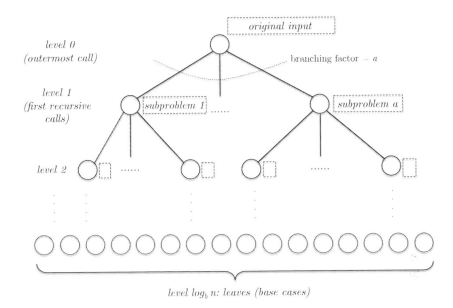

Figure 4.1: The recursion tree corresponding to a standard recurrence. Nodes correspond to recursive calls. Level 0 corresponds to the outermost call, level 1 to its recursive calls, and so on.

Quiz 4.4

What is the pattern? Fill in the blanks in the following statement: at each level $j = 0, 1, 2, \ldots$ of the recursion tree, there are [blank] subproblems, each operating on a subarray of length [blank].

a) a^j and n/a^j, respectively

b) a^j and n/b^j, respectively

c) b^j and n/a^j, respectively

d) b^j and n/b^j, respectively

(See Section 4.4.10 for the solution and discussion.)

4.4.3   Work Performed at a Single Level

Inspired by our MergeSort analysis, the plan is to count the total
number of operations performed by the level-j subproblems in a divide-
and-conquer algorithm, and then add up over all the levels. So zoom
in on a recursion level j. By the solution to Quiz 4.4, there are a^j
different subproblems at level j, each with an input with size n/b^j.
We care only about the size of a subproblem inasmuch as it determines
the amount of work the recursive call performs. Our recurrence (4.3)
asserts that the work performed in a level-j subproblem, not counting
the work performed in its recursive calls, is at most a constant times
the input size raised to the d power: $c(n/b^j)^d$. Adding up over all a^j
of the level-j subproblems gives an upper bound on the amount of
work performed at level j of the recursion tree:

$$\text{work at level } j \leq \underbrace{a^j}_{\#\text{ of subproblems}} \cdot \overbrace{c \cdot \underbrace{\left[\frac{n}{b^j}\right]^d}_{\substack{\text{input} \\ \text{size}}}}^{\text{work per subproblem}} .$$

Let's simplify this expression by separating out the parts that depend
on the level j and the parts that don't:

$$\text{work at level } j \leq cn^d \cdot \left[\frac{a}{b^d}\right]^j .$$

The right-hand side marks the grand entrance of the critical ratio
a/b^d. Given that the value of a versus b^d is exactly what dictates the
relevant case of the master method, we shouldn't be surprised that
this ratio shows up explicitly in the analysis.

4.4.4   Summing over the Levels

How many levels are there? The input size is initially n and drops
by a factor of b with each level. Since we're assuming that n is a
power of b and that the base case kicks in when the input size is 1, the
number of levels is exactly the number of times you need to divide n
by b to reach 1, also known as $\log_b n$. Summing over all the levels
$j = 0, 1, 2, \ldots, \log_b n$ we obtain the following inscrutable upper bound
on the running time (using that cn^d is independent of j and can be

yanked out front):

$$\text{total work} \leq cn^d \cdot \sum_{j=0}^{\log_b n} \left[\frac{a}{b^d}\right]^j. \tag{4.4}$$

Believe it or not, we've reached an important milestone in the proof of the master method. The right-hand side of (4.4) probably looks like alphabet soup, but with the proper interpretation, it holds the keys that unlock a deep understanding of the master method.

4.4.5   Good vs. Evil: The Need for Three Cases

Next we'll attach some semantics to the running time bound in (4.4) and develop some intuition about why the running time bounds in the master method are what they are.

Why is the ratio of a vs. b^d so important? Fundamentally, this comparison represents a tug-of-war between the forces of good and the forces of evil. Evil is represented by a, the *rate of subproblem proliferation (RSP)*—with every level of recursion, the number of subproblems explodes by an a factor, and this is a little scary. Good takes the form of b^d, the *rate of work shrinkage (RWS)*—the good news is that with every level of recursion, the amount of work per subproblem decreases by a factor of b^d.[14] The key question then is: which side wins, the forces of good or the forces of evil? The three cases of the master method correspond exactly to the three possible outcomes of this tug-of-war: a draw ($RSP = RWS$), a victory for good ($RSP < RWS$), or a victory for evil ($RSP > RWS$).

To understand this better, spend some time thinking about the amount of work done at each level of a recursion tree (as in Figure 4.1). When is the amount of work performed increasing with the recursion tree level j? When is it decreasing? Is it ever the same at every level?

---

[14]Why b^d instead of b? Because b is the rate at which the *input size* shrinks, and we care about input size only inasmuch as it determines the amount of work performed. For example, in a divide-and-conquer algorithm with a quadratic-time combine step ($d = 2$), when the input size is cut in half ($b = 2$), only 25% as much work is needed to solve each smaller subproblem (since $b^d = 4$).

Quiz 4.5

Which of the following statements are true? (Choose all that apply.)

  a) If $RSP < RWS$ then the amount of work performed is decreasing with the recursion level j.

  b) If $RSP > RWS$ then the amount of work performed is increasing with the recursion level j.

  c) No conclusions can be drawn about how the amount of work varies with the recursion level j unless $RSP = RWS$.

  d) If $RSP = RWS$ then the amount of work performed is the same at every recursion level.

(See Section 4.4.10 for the solution and discussion.)

4.4.6   Forecasting the Running Time Bounds

We now understand why the master method has three cases. There are three fundamentally different types of recursion trees—with the work-per-level staying the same, decreasing, or increasing—and the relative sizes of a (the RSP) and b^d (the RWS) determine the recursion tree type of a divide-and-conquer algorithm.

Even better, we now have enough intuition to accurately forecast the running time bounds that appear in the master method. Consider the first case, when $a = b^d$ and the algorithm performs the same amount of work at every level of its recursion tree. We certainly know how much work is done at the root, in level 0—$O(n^d)$, as explicitly specified in the recurrence. With $O(n^d)$ work per level, and with $1 + \log_b n = O(\log n)$ levels, we should expect a running time bound of $O(n^d \log n)$ in this case (cf., case 1 of Theorem 4.1).[15]

In the second case, $a < b^d$ and the forces of good are victorious—the amount of work performed is decreasing with the level. Thus more work is done at level 0 than at any other level. The simplest and best outcome we could hope for is that the work done at the root

---

[15]The abbreviation "cf." stands for *confer* and means "compare to."

dominates the running time of the algorithm. Since $O(n^d)$ work is done at the root, this best-case scenario would translate to an overall running time of $O(n^d)$ (cf., case 2 of Theorem 4.1).

In the third case, when subproblems proliferate even faster than the work-per-subproblem shrinks, the amount of work performed is increasing with the recursion level, with the most work being done at the leaves of the tree. Again, the simplest- and best-case scenario would be that the running time is dominated by the work done at the leaves. A leaf corresponds to a recursive call where the base case is triggered, so the algorithm performs only $O(1)$ operations per leaf. How many leaves are there? From the solution to Quiz 4.4, we know that there are a^j nodes at each level j. The leaves are at the last level $j = \log_b n$, so there are $a^{\log_b n}$ leaves. Thus, the best-case scenario translates to a running time bound of $O(a^{\log_b n})$.

The remaining mystery is the connection between our forecast running time bound for the third case of the master method ($O(a^{\log_b n})$) and the actual bound that appears in Theorem 4.1 ($O(n^{\log_b a})$). The connection is... they are exactly the same! The identity

$$\underbrace{a^{\log_b n}}_{\text{more intuitive}} = \underbrace{n^{\log_b a}}_{\text{easier to apply}}$$

probably looks like a rookie mistake made by a freshman algebra student, but it's actually true.[16] Thus the running time bound of $O(n^{\log_b a})$ just says that the work performed at the leaves of the recursion tree dominates the computation, with the bound stated in a form convenient for plugging in parameters (as for the integer and matrix multiplication algorithms analyzed in Section 4.3).

4.4.7   The Final Calculations: Case 1

We still need to check that our intuition in the previous section is actually correct, and the way to do this is through a formal proof. The culmination of our previous calculations was the following scary-looking upper bound on the running time of a divide-and-conquer

---

[16]To verify it, just take the logarithm base-b of both sides: $\log_b(a^{\log_b n}) = \log_b n \cdot \log_b a = \log_b a \cdot \log_b n = \log_b(n^{\log_b a})$. (And since $\log_b$ is a strictly increasing function, the only way $\log_b x$ and $\log_b y$ can be equal is if x and y are equal.)

algorithm, as a function of the parameters a, b, and d:

$$\text{total work} \le cn^d \cdot \sum_{j=0}^{\log_b n} \left[\frac{a}{b^d}\right]^j. \tag{4.5}$$

We obtained this bound by zooming in on a particular level j of the recursion tree (with its a^j subproblems and $c(n/b^j)^d$ work-per-subproblem) and then summing up over the levels.

When the forces of good and evil are in perfect equilibrium (i.e., $a = b^d$) and the algorithm performs the same amount of work at every level, the right-hand side of (4.5) simplifies dramatically:

$$cn^d \cdot \sum_{j=0}^{\log_b n} \underbrace{\left[\underbrace{\frac{a}{b^d}}_{=1}\right]^j}_{=1 \text{ for each } j} = cn^d \cdot \underbrace{(1 + 1 + \cdots + 1)}_{1 + \log_b n \text{ times}},$$

which is $O(n^d \log n)$.[17]

4.4.8 Detour: Geometric Series

Our hope is that for the second and third types of recursion trees (decreasing- and increasing-work-per-level, respectively), the overall running time is dominated by the work performed at the most difficult level (the root and the leaves, respectively). Making this hope real requires understanding geometric series, which are expressions of the form $1 + r + r^2 + \cdots + r^k$ for some real number r and nonnegative integer k. (For us, r will be the critical ratio a/b^d.) Whenever you see a parameterized expression like this, it's a good idea to keep a couple of canonical parameter values in mind. For example, if $r = 2$, it's a sum of positive powers of 2: $1 + 2 + 4 + 8 + \cdots + 2^k$. When $r = \frac{1}{2}$, it's a sum of negative powers of 2: $1 + \frac{1}{2} + \frac{1}{4} + \frac{1}{8} + \cdots + \frac{1}{2^k}$.

When $r \ne 1$, there is a useful closed-form formula for a geometric series:[18]

$$1 + r + r^2 + \cdots + r^k = \frac{1 - r^{k+1}}{1 - r}. \tag{4.6}$$

---

[17]Remember that since different logarithmic functions differ by a constant factor, there is no need to specify the base of the logarithm.

[18]To verify this identity, just multiply both sides by $1 - r$: $(1 - r)(1 + r + r^2 + \cdots + r^k) = 1 - r + r - r^2 + r^2 - r^3 + r^3 - \cdots - r^{k+1} = 1 - r^{k+1}$.

Two consequences of this formula are important for us. First, when $r < 1$,

$$1 + r + r^2 + \cdots + r^k \leq \frac{1}{1-r} = \text{a constant (independent of } k).$$

Thus *every geometric series with $r < 1$ is dominated by its first term*—the first term is 1 and the sum is only $O(1)$. For example, it doesn't matter how many powers of $\frac{1}{2}$ you add up, the resulting sum is never more than 2.

Second, when $r > 1$,

$$1 + r + r^2 + \cdots + r^k = \frac{r^{k+1} - 1}{r - 1} \leq \frac{r^{k+1}}{r - 1} = r^k \cdot \frac{r}{r - 1}.$$

Thus *every geometric series with $r > 1$ is dominated by its last term*—the last term is r^k while the sum is at most a constant factor $(r/(r-1))$ times this. For example, if you sum up the powers of 2 up to 1024, the resulting sum is less than 2048.

4.4.9   The Final Calculations: Cases 2 and 3

Returning to our analysis of (4.5), suppose that $a < b^d$. In this case, the proliferation in subproblems is drowned out by the savings in work-per-subproblem, and the number of operations performed is decreasing with the recursion tree level. Set $r = a/b^d$; since a, b, and d are constants (independent of the input size n), so is r. Since $r < 1$, the geometric series in (4.5) is at most the constant $1/(1 - r)$, and the bound in (4.5) becomes

$$cn^d \cdot \underbrace{\sum_{j=0}^{\log_b n} r^j}_{=O(1)} = O(n^d),$$

where the big-O expression suppresses the constants c and $1/(1 - r)$. This confirms our hope that, with the second type of recursion tree, the total amount of work performed is dominated by the work done at the root.

For the final case, suppose that $a > b^d$, with the proliferation of subproblems outpacing the rate of work shrinkage per-subproblem.

Set $r = a/b^d$. Since r is now greater than 1, the last term of the geometric series dominates and the bound in (4.5) becomes

$$cn^d \cdot \underbrace{\sum_{j=0}^{\log_b n} r^j}_{=O(r^{\log_b n})} = O(n^d \cdot r^{\log_b n}) = O\left(n^d \cdot \left(\tfrac{a}{b^d}\right)^{\log_b n}\right). \qquad (4.7)$$

This looks messy until we notice some remarkable cancellations. Since exponentiation base-b and the logarithm base-b are inverse operations, we can write

$$(b^{-d})^{\log_b n} = b^{-d \log_b n} = (b^{\log_b n})^{-d} = n^{-d}.$$

Thus the $(1/b^d)^{\log_b n}$ term in (4.7) cancels out the n^d term, leaving us with an upper bound of $O(a^{\log_b n})$. This confirms our hope that the total running time in this case is dominated by the work done at the leaves of the recursion tree. Since $a^{\log_b n}$ is the same as $n^{\log_b a}$, we have completed the proof of the master method. $\mathcal{QED}$

4.4.10   Solutions to Quizzes 4.4–4.5

Solution to Quiz 4.4

Correct answer: (b). First, by definition, the "branching factor" of the recursion tree is a—every recursive call that doesn't trigger the base case makes a new recursive calls. This means the number of distinct subproblems gets multiplied by a with each level. Since there is 1 subproblem at level 0, there are a^j subproblems at level j.

For the second part of the solution, again by definition, the subproblem size decreases by a factor of b with each level. Since the problem size is n at level 0, all subproblems at level j have size n/b^j.[19]

---

[19]Unlike in our `MergeSort` analysis, the fact that the number of subproblems at level j is a^j does not imply that the size of each subproblem is n/a^j. In `MergeSort`, the inputs to the level-j subproblems form a partition of the original input. This is not the case in many of our other divide-and-conquer algorithms. For example, in our recursive integer and matrix multiplication algorithms, parts of the original input are reused across different recursive calls.

Solution to Quiz 4.5

Correct answers: (a),(b),(d). First suppose that $RSP < RWS$, and so the forces of good are more powerful than the forces of evil—the shrinkage in work done per subproblem more than makes up for the increase in the number of subproblems. In this case, the algorithm does less work with each successive recursion level. Thus the first statement is true (and the third statement is false). The second statement is true for similar reasons—if subproblems grow so rapidly that they outpace the savings-per-subproblem, then each recursion level requires more work than the previous one. In the final statement, when $RSP = RWS$, there is a perfect equilibrium between the forces of good and evil. Subproblems are proliferating, but our savings in work-per-subproblem are increasing at exactly the same rate. The two forces cancel out, and the work done at each level of the recursion tree remains the same.

The Upshot

☆ A recurrence expresses a running time bound $T(n)$ in terms of the number of operations performed by recursive calls.

☆ A standard recurrence $T(n) \le aT(\frac{n}{b}) + O(n^d)$ is defined by three parameters: the number a of recursive calls, the input size shrinkage factor b, and the exponent d in the running time of the combine step.

☆ The master method provides an asymptotic upper bound for every standard recurrence, as a function of a, b, and d: $O(n^d \log n)$ if $a = b^d$, $O(n^d)$ if $a < b^d$, and $O(n^{\log_b a})$ if $a > b^d$.

☆ Special cases include an $O(n \log n)$ time bound for MergeSort, an $O(n^{1.59})$ time bound for Karatsuba, and an $O(n^{2.81})$ time bound for Strassen.

☆ The proof of the master method generalizes

the recursion tree argument used to analyze
MergeSort.

☆ The quantities a and b^d represent the forces of
evil (the rate of subproblem proliferation) and
the forces of good (the rate of work shrinkage).

☆ The three cases of the master method correspond to three different types of recursion trees:
those with the per-level work performed the
same at each level (a tie between good and evil),
decreasing with the level (when good wins), and
increasing with the level (when evil wins).

☆ Properties of geometric series imply that the
work done at the root of the recursion tree
(which is $O(n^d)$) dominates the overall running
time in the second case, while the work done
at the leaves (which is $O(a^{\log_b n}) = O(n^{\log_b a})$)
dominates in the third case.

Test Your Understanding

Problem 4.1 *(S)* Recall the master method (Theorem 4.1) and its
three parameters a, b, and d. Which of the following is the best
interpretation of b^d?

  a) The rate at which the total work is growing (per level of recursion).

  b) The rate at which the number of subproblems is growing (per
  level of recursion).

  c) The rate at which the subproblem size is shrinking (per level of
  recursion).

  d) The rate at which the work-per-subproblem is shrinking (per
  level of recursion).

Problem 4.2 *(S)* This and the next two questions will give you
further practice with the master method. Suppose the running

time $T(n)$ of an algorithm is bounded by a standard recurrence with $T(n) \le 7 \cdot T(\frac{n}{3}) + O(n^2)$. Which of the following is the smallest correct upper bound on the asymptotic running time of the algorithm?

a) $O(n \log n)$

b) $O(n^2)$

c) $O(n^2 \log n)$

d) $O(n^{2.81})$

Problem 4.3 Suppose the running time $T(n)$ of an algorithm is bounded by a standard recurrence with $T(n) \le 9 \cdot T(\frac{n}{3}) + O(n^2)$. Which of the following is the smallest correct upper bound on the asymptotic running time of the algorithm?

a) $O(n \log n)$

b) $O(n^2)$

c) $O(n^2 \log n)$

d) $O(n^{3.17})$

Problem 4.4 Suppose the running time $T(n)$ of an algorithm is bounded by a standard recurrence with $T(n) \le 5 \cdot T(\frac{n}{3}) + O(n)$. Which of the following is the smallest correct upper bound on the asymptotic running time of the algorithm?

a) $O(n^{\log_5 3})$

b) $O(n \log n)$

c) $O(n^{\log_3 5})$

d) $O(n^{5/3})$

e) $O(n^2)$

f) $O(n^{2.59})$

Challenge Problems

Problem 4.5 *(S)* Suppose the running time $T(n)$ of an algorithm is bounded by the (non-standard!) recurrence with $T(1) = 1$ and $T(n) \leq T(\lfloor \sqrt{n} \rfloor) + 1$ for $n > 1$.[20] Which of the following is the smallest correct upper bound on the asymptotic running time of the algorithm? (Note that the master method does not apply!)

a) $O(1)$

b) $O(\log \log n)$

c) $O(\log n)$

d) $O(\sqrt{n})$

---

[20]Here $\lfloor x \rfloor$ denotes the "floor" function, which rounds its argument down to the nearest integer.

Chapter 5

QuickSort

This chapter covers `QuickSort`, a first-ballot hall-of-fame algorithm. After giving a high-level overview of how the algorithm works (Section 5.1), we discuss how to partition an array around a "pivot element" in linear time (Section 5.2) and how to choose a good pivot element (Section 5.3). Section 5.4 introduces randomized `QuickSort`, and Section 5.5 proves that its asymptotic average running time is $O(n \log n)$ for n-element arrays. Section 5.6 wraps up our sorting discussion with a proof that no "comparison-based" sorting algorithm can be faster than $O(n \log n)$.

5.1 Overview

Ask a professional computer scientist or programmer to list their top 10 algorithms, and you'll find `QuickSort` on many lists (including mine). Why is this? We already know one blazingly fast sorting algorithm (`MergeSort`)—why do we need another?

On the practical side, `QuickSort` is competitive with and often superior to `MergeSort`, and for this reason is the default sorting method in many programming libraries. The big win for `QuickSort` over `MergeSort` is that it runs *in place*—it operates on the input array only through repeated swaps of pairs of elements, and for this reason needs to allocate only a minuscule amount of additional memory for intermediate computations. On the aesthetic side, `QuickSort` is just a remarkably beautiful algorithm, with an equally beautiful running time analysis.

5.1.1 Sorting

The `QuickSort` algorithm solves the problem of sorting an array, the same problem we tackled in Section 1.4.

Problem: Sorting

Input: An array of n numbers, in arbitrary order.

Output: An array of the same numbers, sorted from smallest to largest.

So if the input array is

3	8	2	5	1	4	7	6

then the correct output array is

1	2	3	4	5	6	7	8

As in our `MergeSort` discussion, for simplicity let's assume that the input array has distinct elements, with no duplicates.[1]

5.1.2 Partitioning Around a Pivot

`QuickSort` is built around a fast subroutine for "partial sorting," whose responsibility is to partition an array around a "pivot element."

Step 1: Choose a pivot element. First, choose one element of the array to act as a *pivot element.* Section 5.3 will obsess over exactly how this should be done. For now, let's be naive and just use the first element of the array (above, the "3").

Step 2: Rearrange the input array around the pivot. Given the pivot element p, the next task is to arrange the elements of the array so that everything before p in the array is less than p, and everything after p is greater than p. For example, with the input array above, here's one legitimate way of rearranging the elements:

---

[1]In the unlikely event that you need to implement `QuickSort` yourself, be warned that handling ties correctly and efficiently is a bit tricky, more so than in `MergeSort`. For a detailed discussion, see Section 2.3 of *Algorithms (Fourth Edition)*, by Robert Sedgewick and Kevin Wayne (Addison-Wesley, 2011).

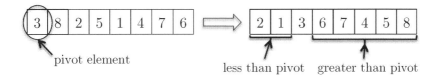

pivot element

less than pivot   greater than pivot

This example makes clear that the elements before the pivot do not need to be placed in the correct relative order (the "1" and "2" are reversed), and similarly for the elements after the pivot. This partitioning subroutine places the (non-pivot) elements of the array into two buckets, one for the elements smaller than the pivot and the other for those greater than the pivot.

Here are the two key facts about this partition subroutine.

Fast.   The partition subroutine has a blazingly fast implementation, running in linear ($O(n)$) time. Even better, and key to the practical utility of `QuickSort`, the subroutine can be implemented in place, with next to no memory beyond that occupied by the input array.[2] Section 5.2 describes this implementation in detail.

Significant progress.   Partitioning an array around a pivot element makes progress toward sorting the array. First, the pivot element winds up in its rightful position, meaning the same position as in the sorted version of the input array (with all smaller elements before it and all larger elements after it). Second, partitioning reduces the sorting problem to two smaller sorting problems: sorting the elements less than the pivot (which conveniently occupy their own subarray) and the elements greater than the pivot (also in their own subarray). After recursively sorting the elements in each of these two subarrays, the algorithm is done![3]

5.1.3   High-Level Description

In the following high-level description of the `QuickSort` algorithm, the "first part" and "second part" of the array refer to the elements less than and greater than the pivot element, respectively:

---

[2]This contrasts with `MergeSort` (Section 1.4), which repeatedly copies elements over from one array to another.

[3]One of the subproblems might be empty, if the minimum or maximum element is chosen as the pivot. In this case, the corresponding recursive call can be skipped.

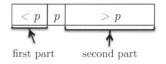

first part   second part

QuickSort (High-Level Description)

Input: array A of n distinct integers.
Postcondition: elements of A are sorted from smallest to largest.

---

if $n \leq 1$ **then**   // base case-already sorted
    return
choose a pivot element p // to-be-implemented
partition A around p // to-be-implemented
recursively sort first part of A
recursively sort second part of A

While both `MergeSort` and `QuickSort` are divide-and-conquer algorithms, the order of operations is different. In `MergeSort`, the recursive calls are performed first, followed by the combine step, `Merge`. In `QuickSort`, the recursive calls occur after partitioning, and their results don't need to be combined at all![4]

5.1.4   Looking Ahead

Our remaining to-do list is:

1. (Section 5.2) How do we implement the partitioning subroutine?

2. (Section 5.3) How should we choose the pivot element?

3. (Sections 5.4 and 5.5) What's the running time of `QuickSort`?

Another question is: "are we really sure that `QuickSort` always correctly sorts the input array?" I've been giving short shrift to formal

---

[4]`QuickSort` was invented by Tony Hoare, in 1959, when he was just 25 years old. Hoare went on to make numerous fundamental contributions in programming languages and was awarded the ACM Turing Award—the equivalent of the Nobel Prize in computer science—in 1980.

correctness arguments thus far because students generally have strong and accurate intuition about why divide-and-conquer algorithms are correct. (Compare this to understanding the running times of divide-and-conquer algorithms, which are usually far from obvious!) If you have any lingering concerns, it is straightforward to formally argue the correctness of QuickSort using a proof by induction.[5]

5.2   Partitioning Around a Pivot Element

Next we fill in the details about how to partition an array around a pivot element p, meaning rearranging the array so that it looks like this:

5.2.1   The Easy Way Out

It's easy to come up with a linear-time partitioning subroutine if we don't care about allocating additional memory. One approach is to do a single scan over the input array A and copy over its non-pivot elements one by one into a new array B of the same length, populating B both from its front (for elements less than p) and its back (for elements bigger than p). The pivot element can be copied into the remaining entry of B after all the non-pivot elements have been

---

[5]Following the template for induction proofs reviewed in Appendix A, let $P(n)$ denote the statement "for every input array of length n, QuickSort correctly sorts it." The base case ($n = 1$) is uninteresting: an array with 1 element is necessarily sorted, and so QuickSort is automatically correct in this case. For the inductive step, fix an arbitrary positive integer $n \geq 2$. We're allowed to assume the inductive hypothesis (i.e., $P(k)$ is true for all $k < n$), meaning that QuickSort correctly sorts every array with fewer than n elements.

After the partitioning step, the pivot element p is in the same position as it is in the sorted version of the input array. The elements before p are exactly the same as those before p in the sorted version of the input array (possibly in the wrong relative order), and similarly for the elements after p. Thus the only remaining tasks are to reorganize the elements before p in sorted order, and similarly for the elements after p. Since both recursive calls are on subarrays of length at most $n - 1$ (if nothing else, p is excluded), the inductive hypothesis implies that both calls sort their subarrays correctly. This concludes the inductive step and the formal proof of correctness for the QuickSort algorithm.

processed. For our running example input array, here's a snapshot from the middle of this computation:

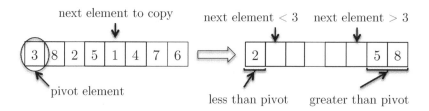

Since this subroutine does only $O(1)$ work for each of the n elements in the input array, its running time is $O(n)$.

5.2.2 In-Place Implementation: The High-Level Plan

How do we partition an array around a pivot element while allocating almost no additional memory? Our high-level approach will be to do a single scan through the array, swapping pairs of elements as needed so that the array is properly partitioned by the end of the pass.

Assume that the pivot element is the first element of the array; this can always be enforced (in $O(1)$ time) by swapping the pivot element with the first element of the array in a preprocessing step. As we scan and transform the input array, we will take care to ensure that it has the following form:

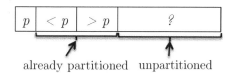

That is, the subroutine maintains the following invariant:[6] the first element is the pivot element; next are the non-pivot elements that have already been processed, with all such elements less than the pivot preceding all such elements greater than the pivot; followed by the not-yet-processed non-pivot elements, in arbitrary order.

If we succeed with this plan, then at the conclusion of the linear scan we will have transformed the array so that it looks like this:

---

[6]An *invariant* of an algorithm is a property that is always true at prescribed points of its execution (like at the end of every loop iteration).

To complete the partitioning, we can swap the pivot element with the last element less than it:

swap

5.2.3   Example

Next we'll step through the in-place partitioning subroutine on a concrete example. It may seem weird to go through an example of a program before you've seen its code, but trust me: this is the shortest path to understanding the subroutine.

Based on our high-level plan, we expect to keep track of two boundaries: the boundary between the non-pivot elements we've already looked at and those we haven't, and within the first group, the boundary between the elements less than the pivot and those greater than the pivot. We'll use the indices j and i, respectively, to keep track of these two boundaries. Our desired invariant can then be rephrased as:

Invariant: all elements between the pivot and i are less than the pivot, and all elements between i and j are greater than the pivot.

Both i and j are initialized to the boundary between the pivot element and the rest. There are then no elements between the pivot and j, and the invariant holds vacuously:

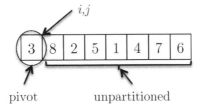

Each iteration, the subroutine looks at one new element, and increments j. Additional work may or may not be required to maintain the invariant. The first time we increment j in our example, we get:

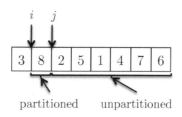

There are no elements between the pivot and i, and the only element between i and j (the "8") is greater than the pivot, so the invariant still holds.

Now the plot thickens. After incrementing j a second time, there is an element between i and j that is less than the pivot (the "2"), a violation of the invariant. To restore the invariant, we swap the "8" with the "2," and also increment i, so that it is wedged between the "2" and the "8" and again delineates the boundary between processed elements less than and greater than the pivot:

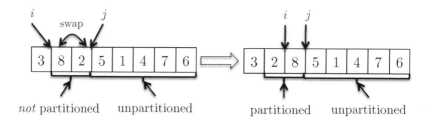

The third iteration is similar to the first. We process the next element (the "5") and increment j. Because the new element is greater than the pivot, the invariant continues to hold and there is nothing more to do:

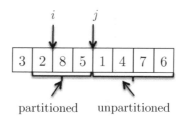

The fourth iteration is similar to the second. Incrementing j ushers in an element less than the pivot (the "1") between i and j, which violates the invariant. But restoring the invariant is easy enough—just swap the "1" with the first element greater than the pivot (the "8"), and increment i to reflect the new boundary between processed elements less than and greater than the pivot:

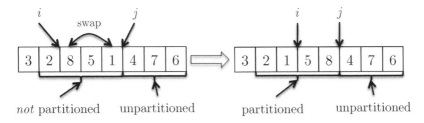

The last three iterations process elements that are larger than the pivot, so nothing needs to be done beyond incrementing j. After all the elements have been processed and everything after the pivot has been partitioned, we conclude with the final swap of the pivot element and the last element smaller than it:

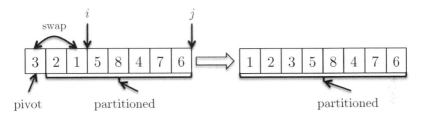

As required, in the final array, all the elements less than the pivot come before it, and all the elements greater than the pivot come after it. It is a coincidence that the "1" and "2" are in sorted order. The elements after the pivot are obviously not in sorted order.

5.2.4   Pseudocode for Partition

The pseudocode for the Partition subroutine is exactly what you'd expect after the example.[7]

---

[7]If you look at other textbooks or on the Web, you'll see a number of variants of this subroutine that differ in the details. (There's even a version performed by Hungarian folk dancers! See https://www.youtube.com/watch?v=ywWBy6J5gz8.) These variants are equally suitable for our purposes.

Partition

Input: array A of n distinct integers, left and right
endpoints $\ell, r \in \{1, 2, \ldots, n\}$ with $l \leq r$.
Postcondition: elements of the subarray
$A[\ell], A[\ell + 1], \ldots, A[r]$ are partitioned around $A[\ell]$.
Output: final position of pivot element.

```
p := A[ℓ]
i := ℓ + 1
for j := ℓ + 1 to r do
    if A[j] < p then        // if A[j] > p do nothing
        swap A[j] and A[i]
        i := i + 1           // restores invariant
    swap A[ℓ] and A[i − 1]   // place pivot correctly
    return i − 1       // report final pivot position
```

The `Partition` subroutine takes as input an array A but operates
only on the subarray of elements $A[\ell], \ldots, A[r]$, where ℓ and r are
given parameters. Looking ahead, each recursive call to `QuickSort`
will be responsible for a specific contiguous subset of the original
input array, and the parameters ℓ and r specify the corresponding
endpoints.

As in the example, the index j keeps track of which elements have
been processed, while i keeps track of the boundary between processed
elements that are less than and greater than the pivot (with $A[i]$ the
leftmost processed element greater than the pivot, if any). Each
iteration of the for loop processes a new element. Like in the example,
when the new element $A[j]$ is greater than the pivot, the invariant holds
automatically and there's nothing to do. Otherwise, the subroutine
restores the invariant by swapping $A[j]$, the new element, and $A[i]$,
the leftmost element greater than the pivot, and incrementing i to
update the boundary between elements less than and greater than
the pivot.[8],[9] The final step, as previously advertised, swaps the pivot

---

[8]No swap is necessary if no elements greater than the pivot have yet been
encountered—the subarray of processed elements is trivially partitioned. But
the extra swap is harmless (as you should verify), so we'll stick with our simple
pseudocode.

[9]Why does this swap and increment always restore the invariant? The invariant

element into its rightful position, displacing the rightmost element less than it. The `Partition` subroutine concludes by reporting this position back to the invocation of `QuickSort` that called it.

This implementation is blazingly fast. It performs only a constant number of operations for each element $A[\ell], \ldots, A[r]$ of the relevant subarray, and so runs in time linear in the length of this subarray. Importantly, the subroutine operates on this subarray in place, without allocating any additional memory beyond the $O(1)$ amount needed to keep track of variables like i and j.

5.2.5   Pseudocode for `QuickSort`

We now have a full description of the `QuickSort` algorithm, modulo the subroutine `ChoosePivot` that chooses a pivot element.

QuickSort

Input: array A of n distinct integers, left and right endpoints $\ell, r \in \{1, 2, \ldots, n\}$.
Postcondition: elements of the subarray $A[\ell], A[\ell+1], \ldots, A[r]$ are sorted from smallest to largest.

---

if $\ell \geq r$ **then**   // 0- or 1-element subarray
   return
$i := \text{ChoosePivot}(A, \ell, r)$ // to-be-implemented
swap $A[\ell]$ and $A[i]$ // make pivot first
$j := \text{Partition}(A, \ell, r)$ // j =new pivot position
$\text{QuickSort}(A, \ell, j-1)$ // recurse on first part
$\text{QuickSort}(A, j+1, r)$ // recurse on second part

---

held before the most recent increment of j (by induction, if you want to be formal about it). This means that all the elements $A[\ell+1], \ldots, A[i-1]$ are less than the pivot and all the elements $A[i], \ldots, A[j-1]$ are greater than the pivot. The only problem is that $A[j]$ is less than the pivot. After swapping $A[i]$ with $A[j]$, the elements $A[\ell+1], \ldots, A[i]$ and $A[i+1], \ldots, A[j]$ are less than and greater than the pivot, respectively. After incrementing i, $A[\ell+1], \ldots, A[i-1]$ and $A[i], \ldots, A[j]$ are less than and greater than the pivot, respectively, which restores the invariant.

Sorting an n-element array A reduces to the function call
QuickSort$(A, 1, n)$.[10]

5.3   The Importance of Good Pivots

Is QuickSort a fast algorithm? The bar is high: simple sorting
algorithms like InsertionSort run in quadratic ($O(n^2)$) time, and
we already know one sorting algorithm (MergeSort) that runs in
$O(n \log n)$ time. The answer to this question depends on how we
implement the ChoosePivot subroutine, which chooses one element
from a designated subarray. For QuickSort to be quick, it's important
that "good" pivot elements are chosen, meaning pivot elements that
result in two subproblems of roughly the same size.

5.3.1   Naive Implementation of ChoosePivot

In our overview of QuickSort we mentioned a naive implementation,
which always picks the first element.

ChoosePivot (Naive Implementation)

Input: array A of n distinct integers, left and right
endpoints $\ell, r \in \{1, 2, \ldots, n\}$.
Output: an index $i \in \{\ell, \ell + 1, \ldots, r\}$.

---

return ℓ

Is this naive implementation already good enough?

Quiz 5.1

What is the running time of the QuickSort algorithm, with
the naive implementation of ChoosePivot, when the n-
element input array is already sorted?

a) $\Theta(n)$

---

[10]The array A is always passed by reference, meaning that all function calls
operate directly on the original copy of the input array.

  b) $\Theta(n \log n)$

  c) $\Theta(n^2)$

  d) $\Theta(n^3)$

(See Section 5.3.3 for the solution and discussion.)

5.3.2   Overkill Implementation of ChoosePivot

Quiz 5.1 paints a worst-case picture of what can happen in QuickSort, with only one element removed per recursive call. What would be the *best-case* scenario? The most perfectly balanced split is achieved by the *median* element of the array, meaning the element for which the same number of other elements are less than it and greater than it.[11] So if we want to work really hard for our pivot element, we can compute the median element of the given subarray.

ChoosePivot (Overkill Implementation)

Input: array A of n distinct integers, left and right
  endpoints $\ell, r \in \{1, 2, \ldots, n\}$.
Output: an index $i \in \{\ell, \ell + 1, \ldots, r\}$.

---

return position of the median element of $\{A[\ell], \ldots, A[r]\}$

We'll see in the next chapter that the median element of an array can be computed in time linear in the array length; let's take this fact on faith for the following quiz.[12] Is there any reward for working hard to compute an ideal pivot element?

Quiz 5.2

What is the running time of the QuickSort algorithm, with

---

[11]For example, the median of an array containing $\{1, 2, 3, \ldots, 9\}$ would be 5. For an even-length array, there are two legitimate choices for the median, and either is fine for our purposes. So in an array that contains $\{1, 2, 3, \ldots, 10\}$, either 5 or 6 can be considered the median element.

[12]You do at this point know an $O(n \log n)$-time algorithm for computing the median of an array. (Hint: Sort!)

the overkill implementation of `ChoosePivot`, on an arbitrary n-element input array? Assume that the `ChoosePivot` subroutine runs in $\Theta(n)$ time.

a) Insufficient information to answer

b) $\Theta(n)$

c) $\Theta(n \log n)$

d) $\Theta(n^2)$

(See Section 5.3.3 for the solution and discussion.)

5.3.3   Solutions to Quizzes 5.1–5.2

Solution to Quiz 5.1

Correct answer: (c). The combination of naively chosen pivots and an already-sorted input array causes `QuickSort` to run in $\Theta(n^2)$ time, which is much worse than `MergeSort` and no better than simple algorithms such as `InsertionSort`. What goes wrong? The `Partition` subroutine in the outermost call to `QuickSort`, with the first (smallest) element as the pivot, does nothing: it sweeps over the array, and since it only encounters elements greater than the pivot, it never swaps any pair of elements. After this call to `Partition` completes, the picture is:

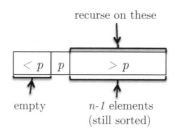

In the non-empty recursive call, the pattern recurs: the subarray is already sorted, the first (smallest) element is chosen as the pivot, and there is one empty recursive call and one recursive call that is passed a subarray of $n - 2$ elements. And so on.

In the end, the `Partition` subroutine is invoked on subarrays of length $n, n - 1, n - 2, \ldots, 2$. Since the work done in one call to

Partition is proportional to the length of the call's subarray, the total amount of work done by QuickSort in this case is proportional to

$$\underbrace{n + (n-1) + (n-2) + \cdots + 1}_{=\Theta(n^2)}$$

and hence is quadratic in the input length n.[13]

Solution to Quiz 5.2

Correct answer: (c). In this best-case scenario, QuickSort runs in $\Theta(n \log n)$ time. The reason is that its running time is governed by the exact same recurrence that governs the running time of MergeSort. That is, if $T(n)$ denotes the running time of this implementation of QuickSort on arrays of length n, then

$$T(n) = \underbrace{2 \cdot T\left(\frac{n}{2}\right)}_{\text{since pivot = median}} + \underbrace{\Theta(n)}_{\text{ChoosePivot \& Partition}} .$$

The primary work done by a call to QuickSort outside its recursive calls occurs in its ChoosePivot and Partition subroutines. We're assuming that the former is $\Theta(n)$, and Section 5.2 proves that the latter is also $\Theta(n)$. Since we're using the median element as the pivot element, we get a perfect split of the input array and each recursive call gets a subarray with at most $\frac{n}{2}$ elements:

$\leq 50\%$ of array $\leq 50\%$ of array

Applying the master method (Theorem 4.1) with $a = b = 2$ and $d = 1$ then gives $T(n) = \Theta(n \log n)$.[14]

---

[13]A quick way to see that $n + (n-1) + (n-2) + \cdots + 1 = \Theta(n^2)$ is to note that it is at most n^2 (each of the n terms is at most n) and at least $n^2/4$ (each of the first $n/2$ terms is at least $n/2$).

[14]Technically, we're using here a variant of the master method that works with Θ-notation rather than O-notation, but otherwise is the same as Theorem 4.1.

5.4   Randomized QuickSort

Choosing the first element of a subarray as the pivot takes only $O(1)$ time but can cause QuickSort to run in $\Theta(n^2)$ time. Choosing the median element as the pivot guarantees an overall running time of $\Theta(n \log n)$ but is much more time-consuming (if still linear-time). Can we have the best of both worlds? Is there a simple and lightweight way to choose a pivot element that leads to a roughly balanced split of the array? The answer is yes, and the key idea is to use *randomization*.

5.4.1   Randomized Implementation of ChoosePivot

A *randomized algorithm* is one that "flips coins" as it proceeds, and can make decisions based on the outcomes of these coin flips. If you run a randomized algorithm on the same input over and over, you will see different behavior on different runs. All major programming languages include libraries that make it easy to pick random numbers at will, and randomization is a tool that should be in the toolbox of every serious algorithm designer.

   Why on earth would you want to inject randomness into your algorithm? Aren't algorithms just about the most deterministic thing you can think of? As it turns out, there are hundreds of computational problems for which randomized algorithms are faster, more effective, or easier to code than their deterministic counterparts.[15]

   The simplest way to incorporate randomness into QuickSort, which turns out to be extremely effective, is to always choose pivot elements *uniformly at random*.

ChoosePivot (Randomized Implementation)

Input: array A of n distinct integers, left and right endpoints $\ell, r \in \{1, 2, \ldots, n\}$.
Output: an index $i \in \{\ell, \ell+1, \ldots, r\}$.

---

return an element of $\{\ell, \ell+1, \ldots, r\}$, chosen uniformly at random

---

[15]It took computer scientists a while to figure this out, with the floodgates opening in the mid-1970s with fast randomized algorithms for testing whether or not an integer is prime.

For example, if $\ell = 41$ and $r = 50$, then each of the 10 elements $A[41], \ldots, A[50]$ has a 10% chance of being chosen as the pivot element.[16]

5.4.2   Running Time of Randomized QuickSort

The running time of randomized QuickSort, with pivot elements chosen at random, is not always the same. There is always some chance, however remote, that the algorithm always picks the minimum element of the remaining subarray as the pivot element, leading to the $\Theta(n^2)$ running time observed in Quiz 5.1.[17] There's a similarly remote chance that the algorithm gets incredibly lucky and always selects the median element of a subarray as the pivot, resulting in the $\Theta(n \log n)$ running time seen in Quiz 5.2. So the algorithm's running time fluctuates between $\Theta(n \log n)$ and $\Theta(n^2)$—which occurs more frequently, the best-case scenario or the worst-case scenario? Amazingly, the performance of QuickSort is almost always close to its best-case performance.

Theorem 5.1 (Running Time of Randomized QuickSort)
For every input array of length $n \geq 1$, the average running time of randomized QuickSort is $O(n \log n)$.

The word "average" in the theorem statement refers to the randomness in the QuickSort algorithm itself. Theorem 5.1 does *not* assume that the input array is random. Randomized QuickSort is a general-purpose algorithm (cf., Section 1.6.1): no matter what your input array is, if you run the algorithm on it over and over again, the average running time will be $O(n \log n)$, good enough to qualify as a for-free primitive. In principle randomized QuickSort can run in $\Theta(n^2)$ time, but you will almost always observe a running time of $O(n \log n)$ in practice. Two added bonuses: the constant hidden in the big-O notation in Theorem 5.1 is reasonably small (like in MergeSort), and the algorithm doesn't spend time allocating and managing additional memory (unlike MergeSort).

---

[16]Another equally useful way is to randomly shuffle the input array in a preprocessing step and then run the naive implementation of QuickSort.

[17]For even modest values of n, there's a bigger probability that you'll be struck by a meteor while reading this!

5.4.3   Intuition: Why Are Random Pivots Good?

To understand deeply why QuickSort is so quick, there's no substitute
for studying the proof of Theorem 5.1, which is explained in Section 5.5.
In preparation for that proof, and also as a consolation prize for the
reader who is too time-limited to absorb Section 5.5, we next develop
intuition about why Theorem 5.1 should be true.

The first insight is that, to achieve a running time of $O(n \log n)$
as in the best-case scenario of Quiz 5.2, it's overkill to use the median
element as the pivot element. Suppose we instead use an "approximate
median," meaning some element that gives us a 25%-75% split or
better. Equivalently, this is an element that is greater than at least
25% of the other elements and also less than at least 25% of the other
elements. The picture after partitioning around such a pivot element
is:

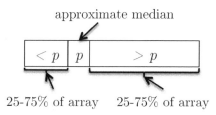

If every recursive call chooses a pivot element that is an approxi-
mate median in this sense, the running time of QuickSort is still
$O(n \log n)$. We cannot derive this fact directly from the master method
(Theorem 4.1), because using a non-median results in subproblems
with different sizes. But it is not hard to generalize the analysis of
MergeSort (Section 1.5) so that it also applies here.[18]

---

[18]Draw out the recursion tree of the algorithm. Whenever QuickSort calls
itself recursively on two subproblems, the subproblems involve different elements
(those less than the pivot, and those greater than it). This means that, for every
recursion level j, there are no overlaps between the subarrays of different level-j
subproblems, and so the sum of subarray lengths of level-j subproblems is at
most n. The total work done at this level (by calls to Partition) is linear in
the sum of the subarray lengths. Thus, like MergeSort, the algorithm does $O(n)$
work per recursion level. How many levels are there? With pivot elements that
are approximate medians, at most 75% of the elements are passed to the same
recursive call, and so the subproblem size drops by at least a factor of 4/3 with
each level. This means there are at most $\log_{4/3} n = O(\log n)$ levels in the recursion
tree, and so $O(n \log n)$ work is done in all.

The second insight is that while you'd have to get incredibly lucky to choose the median element in randomized QuickSort (only a 1 in n chance), you have to be only slightly lucky to choose an approximate median. For example, consider an array that contains the elements $\{1, 2, 3, \ldots, 100\}$. Any number between 26 and 75, inclusive, is an approximate median, with at least 25 elements less than it and 25 elements greater than it. This is 50% of the numbers in the array! So QuickSort has a 50-50 chance of randomly choosing an approximate median, as if it were trying to guess the outcome of a fair coin flip. This means we expect roughly 50% of the calls to QuickSort to use approximate medians, and we can hope that the $O(n \log n)$ running time analysis in the previous paragraph continues to hold, perhaps with twice as many levels as before.

Make no mistake: this is not a formal proof, just a heuristic argument that Theorem 5.1 might plausibly be true. If I were you, given the central position of QuickSort in the design and analysis of algorithms, I would demand an indisputable argument that Theorem 5.1 really is true.

*5.5   Analysis of Randomized QuickSort

Randomized QuickSort seems like a great idea, but how do we really know it will work well? More generally, when you come up with a new algorithm in your own work, how do you know whether it's brilliant or whether it stinks? One useful but ad hoc approach is to code up the algorithm and try it on a bunch of different inputs. Another approach is to develop intuition about why the algorithm should work well, as in Section 5.4.3 for randomized QuickSort. But thoroughly understanding what makes an algorithm good or bad often requires mathematical analysis. This section will give you such an understanding of why QuickSort is so quick.

This section assumes familiarity with the concepts from discrete probability that are reviewed in Appendix B: sample spaces, events, random variables, expectation, and linearity of expectation.

5.5.1   Preliminaries

Theorem 5.1 asserts that for every input array of length $n \geq 1$, the average running time of randomized QuickSort (with pivot elements chosen uniformly at random) is $O(n \log n)$. Let's begin by translating this assertion into a formal statement in the language of discrete probability.

Fix for the rest of the analysis an arbitrary input array A of length n. Recall that a sample space is the set of all possible outcomes of some random process. In randomized QuickSort, all the randomness is in the random choices of pivot elements in the different recursive calls. Thus we take the sample space Ω as the set of all possible outcomes of random choices in QuickSort (i.e., all pivot sequences).

Recall that a random variable is a numerical measurement of the outcome of a random process—a real-valued function defined on Ω. The random variable we care about is the number RT of primitive operations (i.e., lines of code) performed by randomized QuickSort. This is a well-defined random variable because, whenever all the pivot element choices are pre-determined (i.e., $\omega \in \Omega$ is fixed), QuickSort has some fixed running time $RT(\omega)$. Ranging over all possible choices ω, $RT(\omega)$ ranges from $\Theta(n \log n)$ to $\Theta(n^2)$ (see Section 5.3).

We can get away with analyzing a simpler random variable that counts only comparisons and ignores the other types of primitive operations performed. Let C denote the random variable equal to the number of comparisons between pairs of input elements performed by QuickSort with a given sequence of pivot choices. Looking back over the pseudocode, we see that these comparisons occur in exactly one place: the line "if $A[j] < p$" in the Partition subroutine (Section 5.2.4), which compares the current pivot element to some other element of the input subarray.

The following lemma shows that comparisons dominate the overall running time of QuickSort, meaning that the latter is larger than the former only by a constant factor. This implies that, to prove an upper bound of $O(n \log n)$ on the expected running time of QuickSort, we only need to prove an upper bound of $O(n \log n)$ on the expected number of comparisons made.

Lemma 5.2 *There is a constant $a > 0$ such that, for every input array A of length at least 2 and every pivot sequence ω, $RT(\omega) \leq a \cdot C(\omega)$.*

We include the proof for the skeptics; skip it if you find Lemma 5.2 intuitively obvious.

Proof of Lemma 5.2: First, in every call to `Partition`, the pivot element is compared exactly once to every other element in the given subarray. Thus the number of comparisons in the call is linear in the subarray length and, by inspection of the pseudocode in Section 5.2.4, the total number of operations in the call is at most a constant times this. By inspection of the pseudocode in Section 5.2.5, randomized `QuickSort` performs only a constant number of operations in each recursive call outside the `Partition` subroutine.[19] There are at most n recursive calls to `QuickSort` in all—each input array element can be chosen as the pivot only once before being excluded from all future recursive calls—and so the total work outside calls to `Partition` is $O(n)$. Summing over all the recursive calls, the total number $RT(\omega)$ of operations is at most a constant times the number $C(\omega)$ of comparisons, plus $O(n)$. Since $C(\omega)$ is always at least proportional to n, the additional $O(n)$ work can be absorbed into the constant factor a of the lemma statement, and this completes the proof. $\mathcal{QED}$

The rest of this section concentrates on bounding the expected number of comparisons.

Theorem 5.3 (Comparisons in Randomized `QuickSort`) *For every input array of length $n \geq 1$, the expected number of comparisons between input array elements in randomized `QuickSort` is at most $2(n-1)\ln n = O(n\log n)$.*

By Lemma 5.2, Theorem 5.3 implies Theorem 5.1, with a different constant factor hidden in the big-O notation.

5.5.2   A Decomposition Blueprint

The master method (Theorem 4.1) resolved the running time of every divide-and-conquer algorithm we've studied up to this point, but there are two reasons why it doesn't apply to randomized `QuickSort`.

---

[19]This statement assumes that choosing a random pivot element counts as one primitive operation. The proof remains valid even if choosing a random pivot requires $\Theta(\log n)$ primitive operations (as you should check), and this covers typical practical implementations of random number generators.

First, the running time of the algorithm corresponds to a random recurrence or a random recursion tree, and the master method works with deterministic recurrences. Second, the two subproblems that are solved recursively (elements less than the pivot and elements greater than the pivot) do not generally have the same size. We need a new idea.[20]

To prove Theorem 5.3, we'll follow a decomposition blueprint that is useful for analyzing the expectation of complicated random variables. The first step is to identify the (possibly complicated) random variable Y that you care about; for us, this is the number C of comparisons between input array elements made by randomized QuickSort, as in Theorem 5.3. The second step is to express Y as the sum of simpler random variables, ideally indicator (i.e., 0-1) random variables $X_1, \ldots, X_m$;

$$Y = \sum_{\ell=1}^{m} X_\ell.$$

We are now in the wheelhouse of linearity of expectation, which states that the expectation of a sum of random variables equals the sum of their expectations (Theorem B.1). The third step of the blueprint uses this property to reduce the computation of the expectation of Y to that of the simple random variables:

$$\mathbf{E}[Y] = \mathbf{E}\left[\sum_{\ell=1}^{m} X_\ell\right] = \sum_{\ell=1}^{m} \mathbf{E}[X_\ell].$$

When the X_ℓ's are indicator random variables, their expectations are particularly easy to compute via the definition (B.1):

$$\mathbf{E}[X_\ell] = \underbrace{0 \cdot \mathbf{Pr}[X_\ell = 0]}_{=0} + 1 \cdot \mathbf{Pr}[X_\ell = 1] = \mathbf{Pr}[X_\ell = 1].$$

The final step computes the expectations of the simple random variables and adds up the results.[21]

---

[20]There are generalizations of the master method that address both these issues, but they are somewhat complicated and outside the scope of this book.

[21]The randomized load-balancing analysis in Section B.6 is a simple example of this blueprint in action.

> ## A Decomposition Blueprint
>
> 1. Identify the random variable Y that you care about.
>
> 2. Express Y as a sum of indicator (i.e., 0-1) random variables $X_1, \ldots, X_m$:
>
> $$Y = \sum_{\ell=1}^{m} X_\ell.$$
>
> 3. Apply linearity of expectation:
>
> $$\mathbf{E}[Y] = \sum_{\ell=1}^{m} \mathbf{Pr}[X_\ell = 1].$$
>
> 4. Compute each of the $\mathbf{Pr}[X_\ell = 1]$'s and add up the results to obtain $\mathbf{E}[Y]$.

5.5.3   Applying the Blueprint

To apply the decomposition blueprint to the analysis of randomized QuickSort, we need to decompose the random variable C that we really care about into simpler (ideally 0-1) random variables. The key idea is to break down the total comparison count according to the pair of input array elements getting compared.

To make this precise, let z_i denote the ith-smallest element in the input array, also known as the *ith order statistic*. For example, in the array

$$\boxed{6} \; \boxed{8} \; \boxed{9} \; \boxed{2}$$

z_1 refers to the "2," z_2 the "6," z_3 the "8," and z_4 the "9." Note that z_i does *not* denote the element in the ith position of the (unsorted) input array, but rather the element in this position of the sorted version of the input array.

For every pair of array indices $i, j \in \{1, 2, \ldots, n\}$ with $i < j$, we define a random variable X_{ij} as follows:

for every fixed choice of pivots w, $X_{ij}(w)$ is the number of times the elements z_i and z_j get compared in QuickSort when the pivots are specified by w.

For the input array above, for example, $X_{1,3}$ is the number of times the QuickSort algorithm compares the "2" with the "8." We don't care about the X_{ij}'s per se, except inasmuch as they add up to the random variable C that we do care about.

The point of this definition is to implement the second step of the decomposition blueprint. Since each comparison involves exactly one pair of input array elements,

$$C(w) = \sum_{i=1}^{n-1} \sum_{j=i+1}^{n} X_{ij}(w)$$

for every $w \in \Omega$. The fancy-looking double sum on the right-hand side is just iterating over all pairs (i, j) with $i < j$, and this equation just says that the X_{ij}'s account for all the comparisons made by the QuickSort algorithm.

Quiz 5.3

Fix two different elements of the input array, say z_i and z_j. How many times might z_i and z_j be compared with each other during the execution of QuickSort?

a) exactly once

b) 0 or 1 times

c) 0, 1, or 2 times

d) any number between 0 and $n - 1$ is possible

(See Section 5.5.6 for the solution and discussion.)

The solution to Quiz 5.3 shows that all of the X_{ij}'s are indicator random variables. We can therefore apply the third step of our decomposition blueprint to obtain

$$\mathbf{E}[C] = \sum_{i=1}^{n-1} \sum_{j=i+1}^{n} \mathbf{E}[X_{ij}] = \sum_{i=1}^{n-1} \sum_{j=i+1}^{n} \mathbf{Pr}[X_{ij} = 1]. \qquad (5.1)$$

To compute what we really care about, the expected number $\mathbf{E}[C]$ of comparisons, all we need to do is understand the $\mathbf{Pr}[X_{ij} = 1]$'s! Each of these numbers is the probability that some z_i and z_j are compared to each other at some point in randomized QuickSort, and the next order of business is to nail down these numbers.[22]

5.5.4   Computing Comparison Probabilities

There is a satisfying formula for the probability that two input array elements get compared in randomized QuickSort.

Lemma 5.4 (Comparison Probability) *If z_i and z_j denote the ith and jth smallest elements of the input array, with $i < j$, then*

$$\mathbf{Pr}[z_i, z_j \text{ get compared in randomized } \texttt{QuickSort}] = \frac{2}{j - i + 1}.$$

For example, if z_i and z_j are the minimum and maximum elements ($i = 1$ and $j = n$), then they are compared with probability only $\frac{2}{n}$. If there are no elements with value between z_i and z_j ($j = i + 1$), then z_i and z_j are always compared to each other.

Fix z_i and z_j with $i < j$, and consider the pivot z_k chosen in the first call to QuickSort. What are the different scenarios?

Four QuickSort Scenarios

1. The chosen pivot is smaller than both z_i and z_j ($k < i$). Both z_i and z_j are passed to the second recursive call.

2. The chosen pivot is greater than both z_i and z_j ($k > j$). Both z_i and z_j are passed to the first recursive call.

3. The chosen pivot is between z_i and z_j ($i < k < j$). z_i is passed to the first recursive call, and z_j to the second one.

---

[22]Section B.5 makes a big deal of the fact that linearity of expectation applies even to random variables that are not independent (where knowledge of one random variable tells you something about the others). This fact is crucial for us here, since the X_{ij}'s are not independent. For example, if I tell you that $X_{1n} = 1$, you know that either z_1 or z_n was chosen as the pivot element in the outermost call to QuickSort (why?), and this in turn makes it much more likely that a random variable of the form X_{1j} or X_{jn} also equals 1.

4. The chosen pivot is either z_i or z_j ($k \in \{i, j\}$). The
   pivot is excluded from both recursive calls; the other
   element is passed to the first (if $k = j$) or second (if
   $k = i$) recursive call.

We have two things going for us. First, remember that every
comparison involves the current pivot element. Thus z_i and z_j are
compared in the outermost call to QuickSort if and only if one of
them is chosen as the pivot element (scenario 4). Second, in scenario 3,
not only will z_i and z_j not be compared now, but they will never
again appear together in the same recursive call and so cannot be
compared in the future. For example, in the array

8	3	2	5	1	4	7	6

with $z_i = 3$ and $z_j = 7$, if any of the elements $\{4, 5, 6\}$ are chosen as
the pivot element, then z_i and z_j are sent to different recursive calls
and never get compared. For example, if the "6" is chosen, the picture
is:

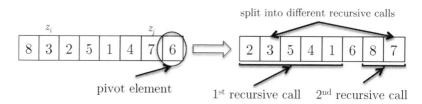

Scenarios 1 and 2 are a holding pattern: z_i and z_j haven't been
compared yet, but it's still possible they will be compared in the
future. During this holding pattern, z_i and z_j, and all of the elements
$z_{i+1}, \ldots, z_{j-1}$ with values in between z_i and z_j, lead parallel lives
and keep getting passed to the same recursive call. Eventually, their
collective journey is interrupted by a recursive call to QuickSort in
which one of the elements $z_i, z_{i+1}, \ldots, z_{j-1}, z_j$ is chosen as the pivot
element, triggering either scenario 3 or scenario 4.[23]

Fast forwarding to this recursive call, which is where the action
is, scenario 4 (and a comparison between z_i and z_j) is triggered if z_i

---

[23] If nothing else, previous recursive calls eventually whittle the subarray down
to just the elements $\{z_i, z_{i+1}, \ldots, z_{j-1}, z_j\}$.

or z_j is the chosen pivot, while scenario 3 (and no such comparison, ever) is triggered if any one of $z_{i+1}, \ldots, z_{j-1}$ is chosen as the pivot. So there are two bad cases (z_i and z_j) out of the $j - i + 1$ options $(z_i, z_{i+1}, \ldots, z_{j-1}, z_j)$. Because randomized `QuickSort` always chooses pivot elements uniformly at random, by symmetry, *each element of $\{z_i, z_{i+1}, \ldots, z_{j-1}, z_j\}$ is equally likely to be the first pivot element chosen from the set.* Putting everything together,

$\mathbf{Pr}[z_i, z_j$ get compared at some point in randomized `QuickSort`]

is the same as

$\mathbf{Pr}[z_i$ or z_j is chosen as a pivot before any of $z_{i+1}, \ldots, z_{j-1}]$,

which is

$$\frac{\text{number of bad cases}}{\text{total number of options}} = \frac{2}{j - i + 1}.$$

This completes the proof of Lemma 5.4. $\mathcal{QED}$

Returning to our formula (5.1) for the expected number of comparisons made by randomized `QuickSort`, we obtain a shockingly exact expression:

$$\mathbf{E}[C] = \sum_{i=1}^{n-1} \sum_{j=i+1}^{n} \mathbf{Pr}[X_{ij} = 1] = \sum_{i=1}^{n-1} \sum_{j=i+1}^{n} \frac{2}{j - i + 1}. \tag{5.2}$$

To prove Theorem 5.3, all that's left to show is that the right-hand side of (5.2) is in fact $O(n \log n)$.

5.5.5   Final Calculations

It's easy to prove an upper bound of $O(n^2)$ on the right-hand side of (5.2): there are at most n^2 terms in the double sum, and each of these has value at most $\frac{1}{2}$ (achieved when $j = i + 1$). But we're after a much better upper bound of $O(n \log n)$, and we'll have to be smarter to get it, by exploiting the fact that most of the quadratically many terms are much smaller than $\frac{1}{2}$.

Consider one of the inner sums in (5.2), for a fixed value of i:

$$\sum_{j=i+1}^{n} \frac{2}{j - i + 1} = 2 \cdot \underbrace{\left(\frac{1}{2} + \frac{1}{3} + \cdots + \frac{1}{n - i + 1} \right)}_{n - i \text{ terms}}.$$

We can bound each of these sums from above by the largest such sum, which occurs when $i = 1$:

$$\sum_{i=1}^{n-1} \sum_{j=i+1}^{n} \frac{2}{j-i+1} \leq \sum_{i=1}^{n-1} \underbrace{\sum_{j=2}^{n} \frac{2}{j}}_{\text{independent of } i} = 2(n-1) \cdot \sum_{j=2}^{n} \frac{1}{j}. \quad (5.3)$$

How big is $\sum_{j=2}^{n} \frac{1}{j}$? Let's look at a picture.

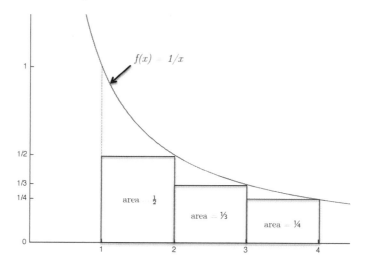

Figure 5.1: Each term of the sum $\sum_{j=2}^{n} 1/j$ can be identified with a rectangle of width 1 (between x-coordinates $j-1$ and j) and height $1/j$ (between y-coordinates 0 and $1/j$). The graph of the function $f(x) = 1/x$ kisses the northeastern corner of each of these rectangles, and so the area under the curve (i.e., the integral) is an upper bound on the area of the rectangles.

Viewing the terms of the sum $\sum_{j=2}^{n} \frac{1}{j}$ as rectangles in the plane as in Figure 5.1, we see that we can bound this sum from above by the area under the curve $f(x) = \frac{1}{x}$ between the points 1 and n, also known as the integral $\int_{1}^{n} \frac{dx}{x}$. If you remember a little bit of calculus, you'll recognize the solution to this integral as the natural logarithm $\ln x$ (i.e., $\ln x$ is the function whose derivative is $\frac{1}{x}$):

$$\sum_{j=2}^{n} \frac{1}{j} \leq \int_{1}^{n} \frac{1}{x} \, dx = \ln x \Big|_{1}^{n} = \ln n - \underbrace{\ln 1}_{=0} = \ln n. \quad (5.4)$$

Chaining together the equations and inequalities in (5.2)–(5.4), we have

$$\mathbf{E}[C] = \sum_{i=1}^{n-1} \sum_{j=i+1}^{n} \frac{2}{j-i+1} \leq 2(n-1) \cdot \sum_{j=2}^{n} \frac{1}{j} \leq 2(n-1) \ln n.$$

Thus the expected number of comparisons made by randomized QuickSort—and also its expected running time, by Lemma 5.2—really is $O(n \log n)$! $\mathcal{QED}$

5.5.6   Solution to Quiz 5.3

Correct answer: (b). If either z_i or z_j is chosen as the pivot element in the outermost call to QuickSort, then z_i and z_j will get compared in the first call to Partition. (Remember that the pivot element is compared to every other element in the subarray.) If i and j differ by more than 1, it is also possible that z_i and z_j never get compared at all (see also Section 5.5.4). For example, the minimum and maximum elements will not be compared to each other unless one of them is chosen as the pivot element in the outermost recursive call (do you see why?).

Finally, as one would expect from a good sorting algorithm, z_i and z_j will never be compared to each other more than once (which would be redundant). Every comparison involves the current pivot element, so the first time z_i and z_j are compared in some call (if ever), one of them must be the pivot element. Since the pivot element is excluded from all future recursive calls, z_i and z_j never again appear together in the same recursive call (let alone get compared to each other).

*5.6   Sorting Requires $\Omega(n \log n)$ Comparisons

Is there a sorting algorithm faster than MergeSort and QuickSort, with running time better than $\Theta(n \log n)$? It's intuitively clear that an algorithm has to look at every input element once, but this implies only a linear lower bound of $\Omega(n)$. This optional section shows that we *can't* do better for sorting—the MergeSort and QuickSort algorithms achieve the best-possible asymptotic running time.

5.6.1   Comparison-Based Sorting Algorithms

Here's the formal statement of the $\Omega(n \log n)$ lower bound.

Theorem 5.5 (Lower Bound for Sorting) *There is a constant*
$c > 0$ *such that, for every* $n \geq 1$, *every comparison-based sorting*
algorithm performs at least $c \cdot n \log_2 n$ *operations on some length-n*
input array.

By a "comparison-based sorting algorithm," we mean an algorithm
that accesses the input array only via comparisons between pairs
of elements, and never directly accesses the value of an element.
Comparison-based sorting algorithms are general-purpose, and make
no assumptions about the input elements other than that they belong
to some totally ordered set. You can think of a comparison-based
sorting algorithm as interacting with the input array through an API
that supports only one operation: given two indices i and j (between 1
and the array length n), the operation returns 1 if the ith element is
smaller than the jth element and 0 otherwise.[24]

For example, the MergeSort algorithm is a comparison-based
sorting algorithm—it doesn't care if it's sorting integers or fruits
(assuming we agreed on a total ordering of all possible fruits, like
alphabetical).[25] So are SelectionSort, InsertionSort, BubbleSort,
and QuickSort.

5.6.2   Faster Sorting Under Stronger Assumptions

The best way to understand comparison-based sorting is to look at
some non-examples. Here are three sorting algorithms that make
assumptions about the input but in exchange beat the $\Omega(n \log n)$
lower bound in Theorem 5.5.[26]

---

[24]For example, the default sorting routine in the Unix operating system works
this way. The only requirement is a user-defined function for comparing pairs of
input array elements.

[25]For an analogy, compare Sudoku and KenKen puzzles. Sudoku puzzles need
only a notion of equality between different objects, and would make perfect sense
with the digits 1–9 replaced by nine different fruits. KenKen puzzles involve
arithmetic and hence need numbers—what would be the sum of a pluot and a
mangosteen?

[26]For a more thorough treatment see, for example, *Introduction to Algorithms
(Third Edition)*, by Thomas H. Cormen, Charles E. Leiserson, Ronald L. Rivest,
and Clifford Stein (MIT Press, 2009).

BucketSort.   The BucketSort algorithm is useful in practice for numerical data, especially when it is spread out uniformly over a known range. For example, suppose the input array has n elements between 0 and 1 that are roughly evenly spread out. In our minds, we divide the interval $[0, 1]$ into n "buckets," the first reserved for input elements between 0 and $\frac{1}{n}$, the second for elements between $\frac{1}{n}$ and $\frac{2}{n}$, and so on. The first step of the BucketSort algorithm does a single linear-time pass over the input array and places each element in its bucket. *This is not a comparison-based step*—the BucketSort algorithm looks at the actual value of an input element to identify which bucket it belongs to. It matters whether the value of an input element is .17 or .27, even if we hold the relative ordering of the elements fixed.

If the elements are roughly evenly spread out, the population of every bucket is small. The second step of the algorithm sorts the elements inside each bucket separately (for example, using InsertionSort). Provided there are few elements in every bucket, this step also runs in linear time (with a constant number of operations performed per bucket). Finally, the sorted lists of the different buckets are concatenated, from the first to the last. This step also runs in linear time. We conclude that linear-time sorting is possible under a strong assumption on the input data.

CountingSort.   The CountingSort algorithm is a variation on the same idea. Here, we assume that there are only k different possible values of each input element (known in advance), such as the integers $\{1, 2, \ldots, k\}$. The algorithm sets up k buckets, one for each possible value, and in a single pass through the input array places each element in the appropriate bucket. The output array is simply the concatenation of these buckets (in order). CountingSort runs in linear time when $k = O(n)$, where n is the length of the input array. Like BucketSort, it is not a comparison-based algorithm,

RadixSort.   The RadixSort algorithm is an extension of CountingSort that gracefully handles n-element integer input arrays with reasonably large numbers represented in binary (a string of 0s and 1s, or "bits"). The first step of RadixSort considers only the block of the $\log_2 n$ least significant bits of the input numbers, and sorts them accordingly. Because $\log_2 n$ bits can encode only n different values—corresponding to the numbers $0, 1, 2, \ldots, n-1$, written in binary—the CountingSort algorithm can be used to implement this step in linear time. The RadixSort algorithm then re-sorts all the elements using the block of the next-least significant $\log_2 n$ bits, and so on until all the bits of the input have been processed. For this algorithm to sort correctly, it's important to implement the CountingSort subroutine so that it is *stable*, meaning that it preserves the relative order of different elements with the same value.[27]   The RadixSort algorithm runs in linear time provided the input array contains only integers between 0 and n^k for some constant k.

These three sorting algorithms demonstrate how additional assumptions about the input data (like being not-too-large integers) enable techniques beyond comparisons (like bucketing) and algorithms that are faster than $\Theta(n \log n)$ time. Theorem 5.5 states that such improvements are impossible for general-purpose comparison-based sorting algorithms. Let's see why.

5.6.3   Proof of Theorem 5.5

Fix an arbitrary deterministic comparison-based sorting algorithm.[28]

Zero comparisons.   First imagine an algorithm that makes *zero* comparisons. Since the algorithm can only learn about the input through comparisons, it knows absolutely nothing about it. For example, such an algorithm has no idea whether the input is

$$\boxed{1}\,\boxed{2}\,\boxed{3}\,\boxed{4} \quad \text{or} \quad \boxed{4}\,\boxed{3}\,\boxed{2}\,\boxed{1}$$

To be correct in the first case, the algorithm's output array must be the same as the input array. Since the algorithm doesn't know which case it's in, its output array must then also be the same as the (unsorted) input array in the second case. This argument shows that every comparison-based sorting algorithm that makes zero comparisons behaves incorrectly for at least one of these two cases.

---

[27]Not all sorting algorithms are stable. For example, QuickSort is not a stable sorting algorithm (do you see why?).

[28]Similar arguments apply to randomized comparison-based sorting algorithms, and no such algorithm has expected running time better than $\Theta(n \log n)$.

One comparison. Now consider an algorithm that makes *one* comparison—say of the first and second input array elements. Such an algorithm can distinguish between the two cases above, and execute differently in each case. But it still has no clue whether the input is

$$\boxed{1 \mid 2 \mid 3 \mid 4} \quad \text{or} \quad \boxed{1 \mid 2 \mid 4 \mid 3}$$

Because the algorithm executes identically in these two cases, it must be incorrect in at least one of them. If its output array doesn't equal the input array in these cases, then it's incorrect in the first scenario; otherwise, it's incorrect in the second scenario.

Two comparisons. An algorithm that makes *two* comparisons is able to learn something about every element of a length-4 array, for example by comparing the first and second elements and then the third and fourth elements. This still isn't enough, as the algorithm can't tell if the input is

$$\boxed{1 \mid 2 \mid 3 \mid 4} \quad \text{or} \quad \boxed{1 \mid 3 \mid 2 \mid 4}$$

If the algorithm could access the *values* of the input array elements, then it could distinguish between these two inputs. But as a comparison-based algorithm, it learns nothing beyond the facts that the first element is smaller than the second and the third element is smaller than the fourth. The algorithm executes identically in the two cases, and can only be correct in one of them.

k comparisons. Consider the general case of an algorithm that always makes at most k comparisons. The general pattern is: if two different input arrays lead to the same answers to all k comparisons, then the algorithm cannot distinguish between them and it executes identically in both cases. Since there are 2^k possible sets of answers to the algorithm's k comparisons, the algorithm can differentiate between at most 2^k different inputs and execute in at most 2^k different ways (Figure 5.2).

There are $n! = n \cdot (n-1) \cdots 2 \cdot 1$ different length-n input arrays that contain the numbers $\{1, 2, 3 \ldots, n\}$, and a correct sorting algorithm

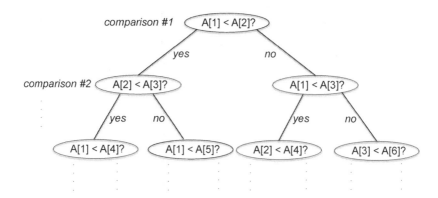

Figure 5.2: A comparison-based sorting algorithm that makes at most k comparisons can execute in at most 2^k different ways.

must differentiate all of them.[29] Thus the maximum number k of comparisons made by a correct comparison-based sorting algorithm must satisfy

$$2^k \geq \underbrace{n!}_{n \cdot (n-1) \cdots 2 \cdot 1} \geq \left(\frac{n}{2}\right)^{n/2},$$

where we have used the fact that the first $n/2$ terms of $n \cdot (n-1) \cdots 2 \cdot 1$ are all at least $\frac{n}{2}$. Taking the logarithm base-2 of both sides shows that

$$k \geq \frac{n}{2} \log_2 \left(\frac{n}{2}\right) = \Omega(n \log n).$$

This completes the proof of Theorem 5.5. $\mathcal{QED}$

The Upshot

★ The famous QuickSort algorithm has three high-level steps: first, it chooses one element p of the input array to act as a "pivot element"; second, its Partition subroutine rearranges the array so that elements smaller than and greater than p come before it and after it, respectively;

---

[29]There are n choices for the location of the "1," $n-1$ remaining choices for the location of the "2," and so on.

third, it recursively sorts the two subarrays on either side of the pivot.

☆ The Partition subroutine can be implemented to run in linear time and in place, meaning with negligible additional memory. As a consequence, QuickSort also runs in place.

☆ The correctness of the QuickSort algorithm does not depend on how pivot elements are chosen, but its running time does.

☆ The worst-case scenario is a running time of $\Theta(n^2)$, where n is the length of the input array. This occurs when the input array is already sorted and the first element is always used as the pivot element. The best-case scenario is a running time of $\Theta(n \log n)$. This occurs when the median element is always used as the pivot.

☆ In randomized QuickSort, the pivot element is always chosen uniformly at random. Its running time can be anywhere from $\Theta(n \log n)$ to $\Theta(n^2)$, depending on its random coin flips.

☆ The average running time of randomized QuickSort is $\Theta(n \log n)$, only a small constant factor worse than its best-case running time.

☆ Intuitively, choosing a random pivot is a good idea because there's a 50% chance of getting a 25%-75% or better split of the input array.

☆ The formal analysis uses a decomposition blueprint to express a complicated random variable as a sum of 0-1 random variables and then apply linearity of expectation.

☆ The key insight is that the ith- and jth-smallest elements of the input array get compared in

> `QuickSort` if and only if one of them is chosen as a pivot before an element with value strictly in between them is chosen as a pivot.
>
> ☆ A comparison-based sorting algorithm is a general-purpose algorithm that accesses the input array only by comparing pairs of elements, and never directly uses the value of an element.
>
> ☆ No comparison-based sorting algorithm has a worst-case asymptotic running time better than $O(n \log n)$.

Test Your Understanding

Problem 5.1 *(S)* Recall the `Partition` subroutine employed by `QuickSort` (Section 5.2). You are told that the following array has just been partitioned around some pivot element:

3	1	2	4	5	8	7	6	9

Which of the elements could have been the pivot element? (List all that apply; there could be more than one possibility.)

Problem 5.2 Let α be some constant, independent of the input array length n, strictly between 0 and $\frac{1}{2}$. What is the probability that, with a randomly chosen pivot element, the `Partition` subroutine produces a split in which the size of both the resulting subproblems is at least α times the size of the original array?

a) α

b) $1 - \alpha$

c) $1 - 2\alpha$

d) $2 - 2\alpha$

Problem 5.3 Let α be some constant, independent of the input array length n, strictly between 0 and $\frac{1}{2}$. Assume you achieve the approximately balanced splits from the preceding problem in every recursive call—so whenever a recursive call is given an array of length k, each of its two recursive calls is passed a subarray with length between αk and $(1-\alpha)k$. How many successive recursive calls can occur before triggering the base case? Equivalently, which levels of the algorithm's recursion tree can contain leaves? Express your answer as a range of possible numbers d, from the minimum to the maximum number of recursive calls that might be needed. [Hint: The formula that relates logarithmic functions with different bases is $\log_b n = \frac{\ln n}{\ln b}$.]

a) $0 \le d \le -\frac{\ln n}{\ln \alpha}$

b) $-\frac{\ln n}{\ln \alpha} \le d \le -\frac{\ln n}{\ln(1-\alpha)}$

c) $-\frac{\ln n}{\ln(1-\alpha)} \le d \le -\frac{\ln n}{\ln \alpha}$

d) $-\frac{\ln n}{\ln(1-2\alpha)} \le d \le -\frac{\ln n}{\ln(1-\alpha)}$

Problem 5.4 *(S)* Define the recursion depth of `QuickSort` as the maximum number of successive recursive calls it makes before hitting the base case—equivalently, the largest level of its recursion tree. In randomized `QuickSort`, the recursion depth is a random variable, depending on the pivots chosen. What are the minimum- and maximum-possible recursion depths of randomized `QuickSort`?

a) minimum: $\Theta(1)$; maximum: $\Theta(n)$

b) minimum: $\Theta(\log n)$; maximum: $\Theta(n)$

c) minimum: $\Theta(\log n)$; maximum: $\Theta(n \log n)$

d) minimum: $\Theta(\sqrt{n})$; maximum: $\Theta(n)$

Challenge Problems

Problem 5.5 Extend the $\Omega(n \log n)$ lower bound in Section 5.6 to apply also to the expected running time of randomized comparison-based sorting algorithms.

Programming Problems

Problem 5.6 Implement the `QuickSort` algorithm in your favorite programming language. Experiment with the performance of different ways of choosing the pivot element.

One approach is to keep track of the number of comparisons between input array elements made by `QuickSort`.[30] For several different input arrays, determine the number of comparisons made with the following implementations of the `ChoosePivot` subroutine:

1. Always use the first element as the pivot.

2. Always use the last element as the pivot.

3. Use a random element as the pivot. (In this case you should run the algorithm 10 times on a given input array and average the results.)

4. Use the *median-of-three* as the pivot element. The goal of this rule is to do a little extra work to get much better performance on input arrays that are nearly sorted or reverse sorted.

   In more detail, this implementation of `ChoosePivot` considers the first, middle, and final elements of the given array. (For an array with even length $2k$, use the kth element for the "middle" one.) It then identifies which of these three elements is the median (i.e., the one whose value is in between the other two), and returns this as the pivot.[31]

   For example, with the input array

8	3	2	5	1	4	7	6

---

[30]There's no need to count the comparisons one by one. When there is a recursive call on a subarray of length m, you can simply add $m-1$ to your running total of comparisons. (Recall that the pivot element is compared to each of the other $m-1$ elements in the subarray in this recursive call.)

[31]A careful analysis would keep track of the comparisons made in identifying the median of the three candidate elements, in addition to the comparisons made in calls to `Partition`.

the subroutine would consider the first (8), middle (5), and last (6) elements. It would return 6, the median of the set $\{5, 6, 8\}$, as the pivot element.

See www.algorithmsilluminated.org for test cases and challenge data sets.

Chapter 6

Linear-Time Selection

This chapter studies the *selection problem*, where the goal is to identify the ith-smallest element of an unsorted array. It's easy to solve this problem in $O(n \log n)$ time using sorting, but we can do better. Section 6.1 describes an extremely practical randomized algorithm, very much in the spirit of randomized `QuickSort`, that runs in *linear* time on average. Section 6.2 provides the elegant analysis of this algorithm—there's a cool way to think about the progress the algorithm makes in terms of a simple coin-flipping experiment, and then linearity of expectation (yes, it's back. . .) seals the deal.

Theoretically inclined readers might wonder whether the selection problem can be solved in linear time without resorting to randomization. Section 6.3 describes a famous deterministic algorithm for the problem, one that has more Turing Award-winning authors than any other algorithm I know of. It is deterministic (i.e., no randomization allowed) and based on an ingenious "median-of-medians" idea for guaranteeing good pivot choices. Section 6.4 proves the linear running time bound, which is not so easy!

This chapter assumes that you remember the `Partition` subroutine from Section 5.2 that partitions an array around a pivot element in linear time, as well as the intuition for what makes a pivot element good or bad (Section 5.3).

6.1 The `RSelect` Algorithm

6.1.1 The Selection Problem

In the *selection problem*, the input is the same as for the sorting problem—an array of n numbers—along with an integer $i \in \{1, 2, \ldots, n\}$. The goal is to identify the ith *order statistic*—the ith-smallest entry in the array.

> ### Problem: Selection
>
> **Input:** An array of n numbers, in arbitrary order, and an integer $i \in \{1, 2, \ldots, n\}$.
>
> **Output:** The ith-smallest element of A.

As usual, we assume for simplicity that the input array has distinct elements, with no duplicates.

For example, if the input array is

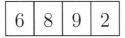

and the value of i is 2, the correct output is 6. If i were 3, the correct output would be 8, and so on.

When $i = 1$, the selection problem is just the problem of computing the minimum element of an array. This is easy to do in linear time—make one pass through the array and remember the smallest element seen. Similarly, the case of finding the maximum element ($i = n$) is easy. But what about for values of i in the middle? For example, what if we want to compute the middle element—the *median*—of an array?

To be precise, for an array with odd length n, the median is the ith order statistic with $i = (n+1)/2$. For an array with even length n, let's agree to define the median as the smaller of the two possibilities, which corresponds to $i = \frac{n}{2}$.[1]

6.1.2   Reduction to Sorting

We already know a fast algorithm for the selection problem, which piggybacks on our fast sorting algorithms.

---

[1]Why would you want to compute the median element of an array? After all, the *mean* (i.e., average) is easy enough to compute in linear time—just sum up all the array elements in a single pass and divide by n. One reason is to compute a summary statistic of an array that is more robust than the mean. For example, one badly corrupted element, such as a data entry error, can totally screw up the mean of an array, but generally has little effect on the median.

Reducing Selection to Sorting

Input: array A of n distinct numbers, and an integer $i \in \{1, 2, \ldots, n\}$.
Output: the ith order statistic of A.

$B := \texttt{MergeSort}(A)$
return $B[i]$

After sorting the input array, we certainly know where to find the ith smallest element—it's hanging out in the ith position of the sorted array. Because MergeSort runs in $O(n \log n)$ time (Theorem 1.2), so does this two-step algorithm.[2]

But remember the mantra of any algorithm designer worth their salt: *can we do better?* Can we design an algorithm for the selection problem that is even faster than $O(n \log n)$ time? The best we can hope for is linear time $(O(n))$—if we don't even take the time to look at each element in the array, there's no hope of always correctly identifying, say, the minimum element. We also know from Theorem 5.5 that any algorithm that uses a sorting subroutine is stuck with a worst-case running time of $\Omega(n \log n)$.[3] So if we *can* get a running time better than $O(n \log n)$ for the selection problem, we'll have proved that *selection is fundamentally easier than sorting.* Accomplishing this requires ingenuity—piggybacking on our sorting algorithms won't cut it.

6.1.3   A Divide-and-Conquer Approach

The randomized linear-time selection algorithm RSelect follows the template that proved so successful in randomized QuickSort: choose a random pivot element, partition the input array around the pivot,

---

[2]A computer scientist would call this a *reduction* from the selection problem to the sorting problem. A reduction absolves you from developing a new algorithm from scratch, and instead allows you to stand on the shoulders of existing algorithms. In addition to their practical utility, reductions are an extremely fundamental concept in computer science, and we will discuss them at length in *Part 4*.

[3]Assuming that we restrict ourselves to comparison-based sorting algorithms, as in Section 5.6.

and recurse appropriately. The next order of business is to understand the appropriate recursion for the selection problem.

Recall what the Partition subroutine in Section 5.2 does: given an array and a choice of pivot element, it rearranges the elements of the array so that everything less than and greater than the pivot appears before and after the pivot, respectively.

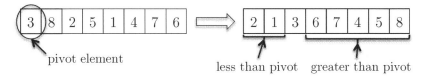

pivot element

less than pivot   greater than pivot

Thus the pivot element ends up in its rightful position, after all the elements less than it and before all the elements greater than it.

QuickSort recursively sorted the subarray of elements less than the pivot element, and also the subarray of elements greater than the pivot. What is the analog for the selection problem?

Quiz 6.1

Suppose we are looking for the 5th order statistic in an input array of 10 elements. Suppose that after partitioning the array, the pivot element ends up in the third position. On which side of the pivot element should we recurse, and what order statistic should we look for?

a) The 3rd order statistic on the left side of the pivot.

b) The 2nd order statistic on the right side of the pivot.

c) The 5th order statistic on the right side of the pivot.

d) We might need to recurse on both the left and the right sides of the pivot.

(See Section 6.1.6 for the solution and discussion.)

6.1.4   Pseudocode for RSelect

Our pseudocode for the RSelect algorithm follows the high-level description of QuickSort in Section 5.1, with two changes. First, we

commit to using random pivot elements rather than having a generic
`ChoosePivot` subroutine. Second, `RSelect` makes only one recursive
call, while `QuickSort` makes two. This difference is the primary
reason to hope that `RSelect` might be even faster than randomized
`QuickSort`.

RSelect

Input: array A of $n \geq 1$ distinct numbers, and an
   integer $i \in \{1, 2, \ldots, n\}$.
Output: the ith order statistic of A.

---

if $n = 1$ **then**   // base case
     return $A[1]$
choose pivot element p uniformly at random from A
partition A around p
$j :=$ p's position in partitioned array
if $j = i$ **then**   // you got lucky!
     return p
else if $j > i$ **then**
     return `RSelect`(first part of A, i)
else   // $j < i$
     return `RSelect`(second part of A, $i - j$)

Partitioning the input array around the pivot element p splits the array
into three pieces, leading to three cases in the `RSelect` algorithm:

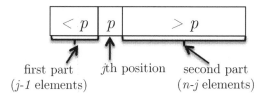

first part jth position   second part
(j-1 elements)   (n-j elements)

Because the pivot element p assumes its rightful position in the
partitioned array, if it's in the jth position, it must be the jth order
statistic. If by dumb luck the algorithm was looking for the jth
order statistic (i.e., $i = j$), it's done. If the algorithm is searching
for a smaller number (i.e., $i < j$), it must belong to the first part
of the partitioned array. In this case, recursing only throws out

elements bigger than the jth (and hence the ith) order statistic, so the algorithm is still looking for the ith-smallest element among those in the first subarray. In the final case $(i > j)$, the algorithm is looking for a number larger than the pivot element, and the recursion mimics the solution to Quiz 6.1. The algorithm recurses on the second part of the partitioned array, throwing out the pivot element and the $j - 1$ elements smaller than it from further consideration. Since the algorithm was originally looking for the ith-smallest element, it's now looking for the $(i - j)$th-smallest element among those that remain.

6.1.5   Running Time of RSelect

Like randomized QuickSort, the running time of the RSelect algorithm depends on the pivots it chooses. What's the worst that could happen?

Quiz 6.2

What is the running time of the RSelect algorithm if pivot elements are always chosen in the worst possible way?

a) $\Theta(n)$

b) $\Theta(n \log n)$

c) $\Theta(n^2)$

d) $\Theta(2^n)$

(See Section 6.1.6 for the solution and discussion.)

We now know that the RSelect algorithm does not run in linear time for all possible choices of pivot elements, but could it run in linear time on average over its random choices of pivots? Let's start with a more modest goal: are there *any* choices of pivots for which RSelect runs in linear time?

What makes a good pivot? The answer is the same as for QuickSort (see Section 5.3): good pivots guarantee that recursive calls receive significantly smaller subproblems. The worst-case scenario is a pivot element that gives the most unbalanced split possible, with one empty subarray and the other subarray having everything save for the pivot element (as in Quiz 6.2). This scenario occurs when the minimum or maximum element is chosen as the pivot. The best-case scenario is a pivot element that gives the most balanced split possible, with two subarrays of equal length.[4] This scenario occurs when the median element is chosen as the pivot. It may seem circular to explore this scenario, as we might well be trying to compute the median in the first place! But it's still a useful thought experiment to understand the best-possible running time that RSelect can have (which had better be linear!).

Let $T(n)$ denote the running time of RSelect on arrays of length n. If RSelect magically chooses the median element of the given subarray in every recursive call, then every recursive call does work linear in its subarray (mostly in the Partition subroutine) and makes one recursive call on a subarray of half the size:

$$T(n) \leq \underbrace{T\left(\frac{n}{2}\right)}_{\text{since pivot = median}} + \underbrace{O(n)}_{\text{Partition, etc.}} .$$

This recurrence is right in the wheelhouse of the master method (Theorem 4.1): since there is one recursive call ($a = 1$), the subproblem size drops by a factor of 2 ($b = 2$), and linear work is done outside the recursive call ($d = 1$), $1 = a < b^d = 2$ and the second case of the master method tells us that $T(n) = O(n)$. This is an important sanity check: if RSelect gets sufficiently lucky, it runs in linear time.

So is the running time of RSelect typically closer to its best-case performance of $\Theta(n)$ or its worst-case performance of $\Theta(n^2)$? With the success of randomized QuickSort under our belt, we might hope that typical executions of RSelect have performance close to the best-case scenario. And indeed, while in principle RSelect can run in $\Theta(n^2)$ time, you will almost always observe a running time of $O(n)$ in practice.

Theorem 6.1 (Running Time of RSelect) *For every input array of length $n \geq 1$, the average running time of RSelect is $O(n)$.*

Section 6.2 provides the proof of Theorem 6.1.

---

[4]We're ignoring the lucky case in which the chosen pivot is exactly the order statistic being searched for—this is unlikely to happen before the last few recursive calls of the algorithm.

Amazingly, the average running time of RSelect is only a constant factor larger than the time needed to read the input! Since sorting requires $\Omega(n \log n)$ time (Section 5.6), Theorem 6.1 shows that selection is fundamentally easier than sorting.

The same comments about the average running time of randomized QuickSort (Theorem 5.1) apply here. The RSelect algorithm is general-purpose in that the running time bound is for arbitrary inputs and the "average" refers only to the random pivot elements chosen by the algorithm. Like with QuickSort, the constant hidden in the big-O notation in Theorem 6.1 is reasonably small, and the RSelect algorithm can be implemented to work in place, without allocating significant additional memory.[5]

6.1.6   Solution to Quizzes 6.1–6.2

Solution to Quiz 6.1

Correct answer: (b). After partitioning the array, we know that the pivot element is in its rightful position, with all smaller numbers before it and larger numbers after it. Since the pivot element wound up in the third position of the array, it is the third-smallest element. We're looking for the fifth-smallest element, which is larger. We can therefore be sure that the 5th order statistic is in the second subarray, and we need to recurse only once. What order statistic are we looking for in the recursive call? Originally we were looking for the fifth-smallest, but now we've thrown out the pivot element and the two elements smaller than it. Since $5 - 3 = 2$, we're now looking for the second-smallest element among those passed to the recursive call.

Solution to Quiz 6.2

Correct answer: (c). The worst-case running time of RSelect is the same as for randomized QuickSort. The bad example is the same as in Quiz 5.1: suppose the input array is already sorted, and the algorithm repeatedly picks the first element as the pivot. In every recursive call, the first part of the subarray is empty while the second

---

[5]The in-place implementation uses left and right endpoints to keep track of the current subarray, like in the pseudocode for QuickSort in Section 5.2.5. See also Programming Problem 6.5.

part has everything save for the current pivot. Thus the subarray length of each recursive call is only one less than the previous one. The work done in each recursive call (mostly by the `Partition` subroutine) is linear in its subarray length. When computing the median element, there are $\approx \frac{n}{2}$ recursive calls, each with a subarray of length at least $\frac{n}{2}$, and so the overall running time is $\Omega(n^2)$.

*6.2   Analysis of `RSelect`

One way to prove the linear expected running time bound for the `RSelect` algorithm (Theorem 6.1) is to follow the same decomposition blueprint that worked so well for analyzing randomized `QuickSort` (Section 5.5), with indicator random variables that track comparisons. For `RSelect`, we can also get away with a simpler instantiation of the decomposition blueprint that formalizes the intuition from Section 5.4.3: (i) random pivots are likely to be pretty good; and (ii) pretty good pivots make rapid progress.

6.2.1   Tracking Progress via Phases

We've already noted that a call to `RSelect` does $O(n)$ work outside of its recursive call, primarily in its call to `Partition`. That is, there is a constant $c > 0$ such that

> (*) for every input array of length n, `RSelect` performs at most cn operations outside of its recursive call.

Because `RSelect` always makes only one recursive call, we can track its progress by the length of the subarray that it is currently working on, which only gets smaller over time. For simplicity, we'll use a coarser version of this progress measure.[6] Suppose the outer call to `RSelect` is given an array of length n. For an integer $j \geq 0$, we say that a recursive call to `RSelect` is in *phase j* if the length of its subarray is between

$$\left(\frac{3}{4}\right)^{j+1} \cdot n \text{ and } \left(\frac{3}{4}\right)^{j} \cdot n.$$

---

[6]A more refined analysis can be done and results in a better constant factor in the running time bound.

For example, the outermost call to `RSelect` is always in phase 0, as are any subsequent recursive calls that operate on at least 75% of the original input array. Recursive calls on subarrays that contain between $(\frac{3}{4})^2 \approx 56\%$ and 75% of the original elements belong to phase 1, and so on. By phase $j \approx \log_{4/3} n$, the subarray has size at most 1 and there are no further recursive calls.

For each integer $j \geq 0$, let X_j denote the random variable equal to the number of phase-j recursive calls. X_j can be as small as 0, since a phase might get skipped entirely, and certainly can't be bigger than n, the maximum number of recursive calls made by `RSelect`. By (*), `RSelect` performs at most

$$c \cdot \underbrace{\left(\frac{3}{4}\right)^j \cdot n}_{\substack{\text{max subarray length} \\ \text{(phase } j)}}$$

operations in each phase-j recursive call. We can then decompose the running time of `RSelect` across the different phases:

$$\text{running time of } \texttt{RSelect} \leq \sum_{j \geq 0} \underbrace{X_j}_{\substack{\# \text{ calls} \\ \text{(phase } j)}} \cdot \underbrace{c \left(\frac{3}{4}\right)^j n}_{\substack{\text{work per call} \\ \text{(phase } j)}}$$

$$= cn \sum_{j \geq 0} \left(\frac{3}{4}\right)^j X_j.$$

This upper bound on the running time of `RSelect` is a complicated random variable, but it is a weighted sum of simpler random variables (the X_j's). Your automatic response at this point should be to apply linearity of expectation (Theorem B.1), to reduce the computation of the complicated random variable to those of the simpler ones:

$$\mathbf{E}[\text{running time of } \texttt{RSelect}] \leq cn \sum_{j \geq 0} \left(\frac{3}{4}\right)^j \mathbf{E}[X_j]. \tag{6.1}$$

So what is $\mathbf{E}[X_j]$?

6.2.2   Reduction to Coin Flipping

We have two things going for us in bounding the expected number $\mathbf{E}[X_j]$ of phase-j recursive calls. First, whenever we pick a pretty good pivot, we proceed to a later phase. As in Section 5.4.3, define an *approximate median* of a subarray as an element that is greater than at least 25% of the other elements in the subarray and also less than at least 25% of the other elements. The picture after partitioning around such a pivot element is:

approximate median

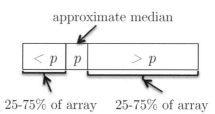

25-75% of array   25-75% of array

No matter which case is triggered in `RSelect`, the recursive call gets a subarray of length at most $\frac{3}{4}$ times that of the previous call, and therefore belongs to a later phase. This argument proves the following proposition.

Proposition 6.2 (Approximate Medians Make Progress) *If a phase-j recursive call chooses an approximate median, then the next recursive call belongs to phase $j + 1$ or later.*

Second, as proved in Section 5.4.3, a recursive call has a decent chance of picking an approximate median.

Proposition 6.3 (Approximate Medians Are Abundant) *A call to `RSelect` chooses an approximate median with probability at least 50%.*

For example, in an array that contains the elements $\{1, 2, \ldots, 100\}$, each of the fifty elements between 26 and 75, inclusive, is an approximate median.

Propositions 6.2 and 6.3 let us substitute a simple coin-flipping experiment for the number of phase-j recursive calls. Suppose you have a fair coin, equally likely to be heads or tails. Flip the coin repeatedly, stopping the first time you get "heads," and let N be the number of coin flips performed (including the last flip). Think of "heads" as corresponding to choosing an approximate median (and ending the experiment).

Proposition 6.4 (Reduction to Coin Flipping) *For each phase* j, $\mathbf{E}[X_j] \le \mathbf{E}[N]$.

Proof: All the differences between the definitions of X_j and N are such that the expected value of the former can only be smaller:

1. There might be no phase-j recursive calls (if the phase is skipped entirely), while there is always at least one coin flip (the first one).

2. Each coin flip has exactly a 50% chance of prolonging the experiment (if it comes up tails). Propositions 6.2 and 6.3 imply that each phase-j recursive call has at most a 50% chance of prolonging the phase—a necessary condition is that it fails to pick an approximate median.

Q.E.D.

The random variable N is a *geometric random variable with parameter* $\frac{1}{2}$. Looking up its expectation in a textbook or on the Web, we find that $\mathbf{E}[N] = 2$. Alternatively, a sneaky way to see this is to write the expected value of N in terms of itself. The key idea is to exploit the fact that the random experiment is memoryless: if the first coin flip comes up "tails," the rest of the experiment is a copy of the original one. In math, whatever the expected value of N might be, it must satisfy the relationship

$$\mathbf{E}[N] = \underbrace{1}_{\text{first flip}} + \underbrace{\frac{1}{2}}_{\mathbf{Pr}[\text{tails}]} \cdot \underbrace{\mathbf{E}[N]}_{\text{further coin flips}} .$$

The unique value for $\mathbf{E}[N]$ that satisfies this equation is 2.[7]

Proposition 6.4 implies that this value is an upper bound on what we care about, the expected number of phase-j recursive calls.

Corollary 6.5 (Two Calls Per Phase) *For every* j, $\mathbf{E}[X_j] \le 2$.

---

[7]Strictly speaking, we should also rule out the possibility that $\mathbf{E}[N] = +\infty$ (which is not hard to do).

6.2.3   Putting It All Together

We can now use the upper bound in Corollary 6.5 on the $\mathbf{E}[X_j]$'s
to simplify our upper bound (6.1) on the expected running time of
RSelect:

$$\mathbf{E}[\text{running time of RSelect}] \le cn \sum_{j \ge 0} \left(\frac{3}{4}\right)^j \mathbf{E}[X_j] \le 2cn \sum_{j \ge 0} \left(\frac{3}{4}\right)^j.$$

The sum $\sum_{j \ge 0} \left(\frac{3}{4}\right)^j$ looks messy, but it's a beast we've already tamed.
When proving the master method (Section 4.4), we took a detour
to discuss geometric series (Section 4.4.8), and derived the exact
formula (4.6):

$$1 + r + r^2 + \cdots + r^k = \frac{1 - r^{k+1}}{1 - r}$$

for every real number $r \ne 1$ and nonnegative integer k. When $r < 1$,
this quantity is at most $\frac{1}{1-r}$, no matter how big k is. Plugging in
$r = \frac{3}{4}$, we have

$$\sum_{j \ge 0} \left(\frac{3}{4}\right)^j \le \frac{1}{1 - \frac{3}{4}} = 4,$$

and so

$$\mathbf{E}[\text{running time of RSelect}] \le 8cn = O(n).$$

This completes the analysis of RSelect and the proof of Theorem 6.1.
$\mathcal{QED}$

*6.3   The DSelect Algorithm

The RSelect algorithm runs in expected linear time for every input,
where the expectation is over the random choices made by the algorithm. Is randomization required for linear-time selection?[8] This
section and the next resolve this question with a deterministic linear-
time algorithm for the selection problem.

For the sorting problem, the $O(n \log n)$ average running time
of randomized QuickSort is matched by that of the deterministic

---

[8]Understanding the power of randomness in computation more generally is a
deep question and continues to be a topic of active research in theoretical computer
science.

MergeSort algorithm, and both QuickSort and MergeSort are useful algorithms in practice. In contrast, while the deterministic linear-time selection algorithm described in this section works OK in practice, it is not competitive with the RSelect algorithm. The two reasons for this are larger constant factors in the running time and the work performed by DSelect allocating and managing additional memory. Still, the ideas in the algorithm are so cool that I can't help but tell you about them.

6.3.1   The Big Idea: Median-of-Medians

The RSelect algorithm is fast because random pivots are likely to be pretty good, yielding a roughly balanced split of the input array after partitioning, and pretty good pivots make rapid progress. If we're not allowed to use randomization, how can we compute a pretty good pivot without doing too much work?

The big idea in deterministic linear-time selection is to use the "median-of-medians" as a proxy for the true median. The algorithm treats the input array elements like sports teams and runs a two-round knockout tournament, the champion of which is the pivot element; see also Figure 6.1.

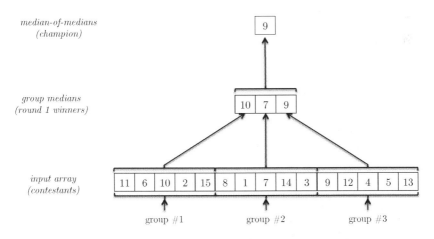

Figure 6.1: Computing a pivot element with a two-round knockout tournament. In this example, the chosen pivot is not the median of the input array, but it is pretty close.

The first round is the group stage, with the elements in positions 1–5 of the input array the first group, the elements in positions 6–10 the second group, and so on. The first-round winner of a group of 5 is defined as the median element (i.e., the third-smallest). Since there are $\approx \frac{n}{5}$ groups of 5, there are $\approx \frac{n}{5}$ first-round winners. (As usual, we ignore fractions for simplicity.) The tournament champion is then defined as the median of the first-round winners.

6.3.2   Pseudocode for DSelect

How do we actually compute the median-of-medians? Implementing the first stage of the knockout tournament is easy, since each median computation involves only 5 elements. For example, each such computation can be done by brute force, (for each of the 5 possibilities, explicitly check if it's the middle element), or by using our reduction to sorting (Section 6.1.2). To implement the second stage, we compute the median of the $\approx \frac{n}{5}$ first-round winners *recursively*.

DSelect

Input: array A of $n \geq 1$ distinct numbers, and an integer $i \in \{1, 2, \ldots, n\}$.
Output: the ith order statistic of A.

---

1 **if** $n = 1$ **then**   // base case
2   return $A[1]$

3 **for** $h := 1$ to $\frac{n}{5}$ **do**   // first-round winners
4      $C[h] :=$ middle element from the hth group of 5
5 $p := \text{DSelect}(C, \frac{n}{10})$ // median-of-medians
6 partition A around p
7 $j := p$'s position in partitioned array
8 **if** $j = i$ **then**   // you got lucky!
9   return p
10 **else if** $j > i$ **then**
11   return DSelect(first part of A, i)
12 **else**   // $j < i$
13   return DSelect(second part of A, $i - j$)

Lines 1–2 and 6–13 are identical to RSelect. Lines 3–5 are the only new part of the algorithm; they compute the median-of-medians of the input array, replacing the line in RSelect that chooses a pivot element at random.

Lines 3 and 4 compute the first-round winners of the knockout tournament, with the middle element of each group of 5 computed using brute force or a sorting algorithm, and copy these winners over into a new array C.[9] Line 5 computes the tournament champion by recursively computing the median of C; since C has length (roughly) $\frac{n}{5}$, this is the $\frac{n}{10}$th order statistic of C. No randomization is used in any step of the algorithm.

6.3.3   Understanding DSelect

It may seem dangerously circular to recursively call DSelect while computing the pivot element. To understand what's going on, let's first be clear on the total number of recursive calls.

Quiz 6.3

How many recursive calls does a single call to DSelect typically make?

a) 0

b) 1

c) 2

d) 3

(See below for the solution and discussion.)

Correct answer: (c). Putting aside the base case and the lucky case in which the pivot element happens to be the desired order statistic, the DSelect algorithm makes two recursive calls. To see why, don't overthink it; just inspect the pseudocode for DSelect line by line. There is one recursive call on line 5, and one more on either line 11 or 13.

---

[9]This auxiliary array is why DSelect, unlike RSelect, fails to run in place.

There are two common points of confusion about these two recursive calls. First, isn't the fact that the RSelect algorithm makes only one recursive call the reason it runs faster than our sorting algorithms? Isn't the DSelect algorithm giving up this improvement by making two recursive calls? Section 6.4 shows that, because the extra recursive call in line 5 needs to solve only a relatively small subproblem (with 20% of the elements of the original array), we can still rescue the linear-time analysis.

Second, the two recursive calls play fundamentally different roles. The goal of the recursive call in line 5 is to identify a good pivot element for the current recursive call. The goal of the recursive call in line 11 or 13 is the usual one, to recursively solve a smaller residual problem left by the current recursive call. Nevertheless, the recursive structure in DSelect is squarely in the tradition of all the other divide-and-conquer algorithms we've studied: each recursive call makes a small number of further recursive calls on strictly smaller subproblems, and does some amount of additional work. If we weren't worried about an algorithm like MergeSort or QuickSort running forever, we shouldn't be worried about DSelect either.

6.3.4   Running Time of DSelect

The DSelect algorithm is not just a well-defined program that completes in a finite amount of time—it runs in *linear* time, performing only a constant factor more work than necessary to read the input.

Theorem 6.6 (Running Time of DSelect) *For every input array of length $n \geq 1$, the running time of DSelect is $O(n)$.*

Unlike the running time of RSelect, which can in principle be as bad as $\Theta(n^2)$, the running time of DSelect is always $O(n)$. Still, you should prefer RSelect to DSelect in practice, because the former runs in place and the constant hidden in the "$O(n)$" average running time in Theorem 6.1 is smaller than the constant hidden in Theorem 6.6.

A Computer Science Superteam

One of the goals of this book series is to make famous algorithms seem so simple (at least in hindsight) that you feel like you could have come up with them yourself, had you been in the right place at the right time. Almost nobody feels this way about the DSelect algorithm, which was devised by a computer science superteam of five researchers, four of whom have been recognized with the ACM Turing Award (all for different things!), the equivalent of the Nobel Prize for computer science.[10] So don't despair if it's hard to imagine coming up with the DSelect algorithm, even on your most creative days—it's also hard to imagine beating Roger Federer (let alone five of him) on the tennis court!

*6.4   Analysis of DSelect

Could the DSelect algorithm really run in linear time? It seems to do an extravagant amount of work, with two recursive calls and significant extra work outside the recursive calls. Every other algorithm we've seen with two or more recursive calls has running time $\Theta(n \log n)$ or worse.

6.4.1   Work Outside Recursive Calls

Let's start by understanding the number of operations performed by a call to DSelect outside its recursive calls. The two steps that require significant work are computing the first-round winners (lines 3–4) and partitioning the input array around the median-of-medians (line 6).

---

[10]The algorithm and its analysis were published in the paper "Times Bounds for Selection," by Manuel Blum, Robert W. Floyd, Vaughan Pratt, Ronald L. Rivest, and Robert E. Tarjan (*Journal of Computer and System Sciences*, 1973). (It was very unusual to see papers with five authors back then.) In chronological order: Floyd won the Turing Award in 1978 for contributions to algorithms and also programming languages and compilers; Tarjan was recognized in 1986 (along with John E. Hopcroft) for his work on algorithms and data structures, which we'll discuss further in later parts of *Algorithms Illuminated*; Blum was awarded it in 1995, largely for his contributions to cryptography; and Rivest, whom you may know as the "R" in the RSA cryptosystem, won it in 2002 (with Leonard Adleman and Adi Shamir) for his work on public-key cryptography. Meanwhile, Pratt is famous for accomplishments that run the gamut from primality testing algorithms to the co-founding of Sun Microsystems!

As in `QuickSort` or `RSelect`, the second step runs in linear time. What about the first step?

Focus on a particular group of 5 elements. Because this is only a constant number of elements (independent of the input array length n), computing the median takes constant time. For example, suppose we do this computation by reducing to sorting (Section 6.1.2), say using `MergeSort`. We understand well the amount of work done by `MergeSort` (Theorem 1.2): at most

$$6m(\log_2 m + 1)$$

operations to sort an array of length m. You might be worried about the fact that the `MergeSort` algorithm does not run in linear time. But we're invoking it only for constant-size subarrays ($m = 5$), and as a result it performs a constant number of operations (at most $6 \cdot 5 \cdot (\log_2 5 + 1) \leq 120$) per subarray. Summing over the $\frac{n}{5}$ groups of 5 that need to be sorted, this is at most $120 \cdot \frac{n}{5} = 24n = O(n)$ operations in all. We conclude that, outside its recursive calls, the `DSelect` algorithm does only linear work.

6.4.2   A Rough Recurrence

In Chapter 4 we analyzed divide-and-conquer algorithms using recurrences, which express a running time bound $T(n)$ in terms of the number of operations performed by recursive calls. Let's try the same approach here, letting $T(n)$ denote the maximum number of operations that the `DSelect` algorithm performs on an input array of length n. When $n = 1$ the `DSelect` algorithm just returns the sole array element, so $T(1) = 1$. For larger n, the `DSelect` algorithm makes one recursive call in line 5, another recursive call in line 11 or 13, and performs $O(n)$ additional work (for partitioning, and computing and copying over the first-round winners). This translates to a recurrence of the form

$$T(n) \leq T\underbrace{\left(\text{size of subproblem } \#1\right)}_{=n/5} + T\underbrace{\left(\text{size of subproblem } \#2\right)}_{=?} + O(n).$$

To evaluate the running time of `DSelect`, we need to understand the sizes of the subproblems solved by its two recursive calls. The size of the first subproblem (line 5) is $\frac{n}{5}$, the number of first-round winners.

We don't know the size of the second subproblem—it depends on which element ends up being the pivot, and on whether the order statistic sought is less than or greater than this pivot. This indeterminacy in subproblem size is why we didn't use recurrences to analyze the QuickSort and RSelect algorithms.

In the special case in which the true median element of the input array is chosen as the pivot, the second subproblem is guaranteed to comprise at most $\frac{n}{2}$ elements. The median-of-medians is generally not the true median (Figure 6.1). Is it close enough to guarantee an approximately balanced split of the input array, and hence a not-too-big subproblem in line 11 or 13?

6.4.3   The 30-70 Lemma

The heart of the analysis of DSelect is the following lemma, which quantifies the payoff of the hard work done to compute the median-of-medians: this pivot element guarantees a split of 30%-70% or better of the input array.

Lemma 6.7 (30-70 Lemma) *For every input array of length $n \geq 2$, the subarray passed to the recursive call in line 11 or 13 of DSelect has length at most $\frac{7}{10}n$.*[11]

The 30-70 Lemma lets us substitute "$\frac{7}{10}n$" for "?" in the rough recurrence above: for every $n \geq 2$,

$$T(n) \leq T\left(\frac{1}{5} \cdot n\right) + T\left(\frac{7}{10} \cdot n\right) + O(n). \qquad (6.2)$$

We first prove the 30-70 Lemma, and then prove that the recurrence (6.2) implies that DSelect is a linear-time algorithm.

Proof of Lemma 6.7: Let $k = \frac{n}{5}$ denote the number of groups of 5, and hence the number of first-round winners. Define x_i as the ith-smallest of the first-round winners. Equivalently, $x_1, \ldots, x_k$ are the

---

[11]Strictly speaking, because one of the "groups of 5" could have fewer than five elements (if n is not a multiple of 5), the $\frac{7}{10}n$ should be $\frac{7}{10}n + 2$, rounded up to the nearest integer. We'll ignore the "+2" for the same reason we ignore fractions—it is a detail that complicates the analysis in an uninteresting way and has no real effect on the bottom line.

first-round winners listed in sorted order. The tournament champion, the median-of-medians, is $x_{k/2}$ (or $x_{\lceil k/2 \rceil}$, if k is odd).[12]

The plan is to argue that $x_{k/2}$ is no smaller than at least 60% of the elements in at least 50% of the groups of 5, and is no larger than at least 60% of the elements in at least 50% of the groups. Then at least $60\% \cdot 50\% = 30\%$ of the input array elements would be no larger than the median-of-medians, and at least 30% would be no smaller:

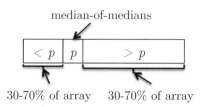

30-70% of array   30-70% of array

To implement this plan, consider the following thought experiment. In our minds (not in the actual algorithm!), we lay out all the input array elements in a two-dimensional grid format. There are five rows, and each of the $\frac{n}{5}$ columns corresponds to one of the groups of 5. Within each column, we lay out the 5 elements in sorted order from bottom to top. Finally, we lay out the columns so that the first-round winners (i.e., the elements in the middle row) are in sorted order from left to right. For example, if the input array is

| 11 | 6 | 10 | 2 | 15 | 8 | 1 | 7 | 14 | 3 | 9 | 12 | 4 | 5 | 13 |

then the corresponding grid is

14		13		15
V		V		V
8		12		11
V		V pivot		V
7	<	9	<	10
V		V		V
3		5		6
V		V		V
1		4		2

---

[12]The notation $\lceil x \rceil$ denotes the "ceiling" function, which rounds its argument up to the nearest integer.

with the pivot element, the median-of-medians, in the center position.

Key Observation

Because the middle row is sorted from left to right, and each column is sorted from bottom to top, *all the elements to the left and down from the pivot are less than the pivot, and all the elements to the right and up from the pivot are greater than the pivot.*[13]

In our example, the pivot is the "9," the elements to the left and down are $\{1, 3, 4, 5, 7\}$, and the elements to the right and up are $\{10, 11, 12, 13, 15\}$. Thus at least 6 elements will be excluded from the subarray passed to the next recursive call—the pivot element 9 and either $\{10, 11, 12, 13, 15\}$ (in line 11) or $\{1, 3, 4, 5, 7\}$ (in line 13). Either way, the next recursive call receives at most 9 elements, and 9 is less than 70% of 15.

The argument for the general case is the same. Figure 6.2 depicts what the grid looks like for an arbitrary input array. Because the pivot element is the median of the elements in the middle row, at least 50% of the columns are to the left of the one that contains the pivot (counting also the pivot's own column). In each of these columns, at least 60% of the elements (the three smallest of the 5) are no larger than the column's median and hence no larger than the pivot element. Thus at least 30% of the input array elements are no larger than the pivot element, and all of these would be excluded from the recursive call in line 13. Similarly, at least 30% of the elements are no smaller than the pivot, and these would be excluded from the recursive call in line 11. This completes the proof of the 30-70 lemma. $\mathcal{QED}$

6.4.4   Solving the Recurrence

The 30-70 Lemma implies that the input size shrinks by a constant factor with every recursive call of DSelect, and this bodes well for a linear running time. But is it a Pyrrhic victory? Does the cost

---

[13]Elements to the left and up or to the right and down could be either less than or greater than the pivot.

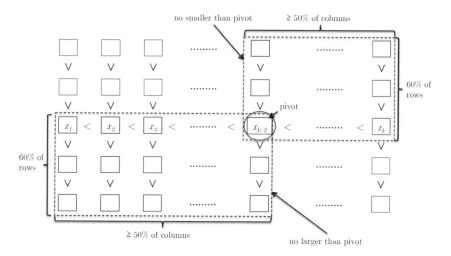

Figure 6.2: Proof of the 30-70 Lemma. Imagine the input array elements laid out in a grid format. Each column corresponds to a group of 5, sorted from bottom to top. Columns are sorted in order of their middle elements. The picture assumes that k is even; for k odd, the "$x_{k/2}$" is instead "$x_{\lceil k/2 \rceil}$." Elements to the southwest of the median-of-medians can only be less than it; those to the northeast can only be greater than it. As a result, at least $60\% \cdot 50\% = 30\%$ of the elements are excluded from each of the two possible recursive calls.

of computing the median-of-medians outweigh the benefits of partitioning around a pretty good pivot? Answering these questions, and completing the proof of Theorem 6.6, requires figuring out the solution to the recurrence in (6.2).

Since the `DSelect` algorithm does $O(n)$ work outside its recursive calls (computing first-round winners, partitioning the array, etc.), there is a constant $c > 0$ such that, for every $n \geq 2$,

$$T(n) \leq T\left(\frac{1}{5} \cdot n\right) + T\left(\frac{7}{10} \cdot n\right) + cn, \qquad (6.3)$$

where $T(n)$ is an upper bound on the running time of `DSelect` on length-n arrays. We can assume that $c \geq 1$ (as increasing c cannot invalidate the inequality (6.3)). Also, $T(1) = 1$. As we'll see, the crucial property of this recurrence is that $\frac{1}{5} + \frac{7}{10} < 1$.

We leaned on the master method (Chapter 4) to evaluate all the recurrences we've encountered so far—for MergeSort, Karatsuba, Strassen, and more, we just plugged in the three relevant parameters (a, b, and d) and out popped an upper bound on the algorithm's running time. Unfortunately, the two recursive calls in DSelect have different input sizes, and this rules out applying Theorem 4.1. It is possible to generalize the recursion tree argument in Theorem 4.1 to accommodate the recurrence in (6.3).[14] For variety's sake, and to add another tool to your toolbox, we proceed instead with a different method.

6.4.5   The Guess-and-Check Method

The *guess-and-check* method for evaluating recurrences is just as ad hoc as it sounds, but it's also extremely flexible and applies to arbitrarily crazy recurrences.

Step 1: Guess.   Guess a function $f(n)$ which you suspect satisfies $T(n) = O(f(n))$.

Step 2:   Check.   Prove by induction on n that $T(n)$ really is $O(f(n))$.

In general, the guessing step is a bit of a dark art. In our case, since we're trying to prove a linear running time bound, we'll guess that $T(n) = O(n)$.[15] That is, we guess that there is a constant $\ell > 0$ (independent of n) such that

$$T(n) \leq \ell \cdot n \tag{6.4}$$

for every positive integer n. If true, since ℓ is a constant, this would imply our hope that $T(n) = O(n)$.

---

[14]For a heuristic argument, think about the first pair of recursive calls to DSelect—the two nodes in level 1 of the algorithm's recursion tree. One has 20% of the input array elements, the other at most 70%, and the work done at this level is linear in the sum of the two subproblem sizes. Thus the amount of work done at level 1 is at most 90% of that done at level 0, and so on at subsequent levels. This resembles the second case of the master method, in which the work-per-level drops by a constant factor each level. This analogy suggests that the $O(n)$ work performed at the root should dominate the running time (cf., Section 4.4.6).

[15]"Hope and check" might be a more apt description for us!

When verifying (6.4), we are free to choose ℓ however we want, as long as it is independent of n. Similar to asymptotic notation proofs, the usual way to figure out the appropriate constant is to reverse engineer it (cf., Section 2.5). Here, we'll take $\ell = 10c$, where c is the constant factor in the recurrence (6.3). (Since c is a constant, so is ℓ.) Where did this number come from? It's the smallest constant for which the inequality (6.5) below is valid.

We prove (6.4) by induction. In the language of Appendix A, $P(n)$ is the assertion that $T(n) \le \ell \cdot n = 10c \cdot n$. For the base case, we need to prove directly that $P(1)$ is true, meaning that $T(1) \le 10c$. The recurrence explicitly says that $T(1) = 1$ and $c \ge 1$, so certainly $T(1) \le 10c$.

For the inductive step, fix an arbitrary positive integer $n \ge 2$. We need to prove that $T(n) \le \ell \cdot n$. The inductive hypothesis states that $P(1), \ldots, P(n-1)$ are all true, meaning that $T(k) \le \ell \cdot k$ for all $k < n$. To prove $P(n)$, let's just follow our noses.

First, the recurrence (6.3) decomposes $T(n)$ into three terms:

$$T(n) \le \underbrace{T\left(\frac{1}{5} \cdot n\right)}_{\substack{\le \ell \cdot \frac{n}{5} \\ \text{(ind. hyp.)}}} + \underbrace{T\left(\frac{7}{10} \cdot n\right)}_{\substack{\le \ell \cdot \frac{7n}{10} \\ \text{(ind. hyp.)}}} + cn.$$

We can't directly manipulate any of these terms, but we can apply the inductive hypothesis, once with $k = \frac{n}{5}$ and once with $k = \frac{7n}{10}$:

$$T(n) \le \ell \cdot \frac{n}{5} + \ell \cdot \frac{7n}{10} + cn.$$

Grouping terms,

$$T(n) \le n \underbrace{\left(\frac{9}{10}\ell + c\right)}_{\substack{= \ell \\ \text{(as } \ell = 10c)}} = \ell \cdot n. \tag{6.5}$$

This proves the inductive step, which verifies that $T(n) \le \ell \cdot n = O(n)$ and completes the proof that the ingenious `DSelect` algorithm runs in linear time (Theorem 6.6). $\mathscr{QED}$

The Upshot

★ The goal in the selection problem is to compute the ith-smallest element of an unsorted array.

★ The selection problem can be solved in $O(n \log n)$ time, where n is the length of the input array, by sorting the array and then returning the ith element.

★ The problem can also be solved by partitioning the input array around a pivot element, as in QuickSort, and recursing once on the relevant side. The RSelect algorithm always chooses the pivot element uniformly at random.

★ The running time of RSelect varies from $\Theta(n)$ to $\Theta(n^2)$, depending on the pivots chosen.

★ The average running time of RSelect is $\Theta(n)$. The proof uses a reduction to a coin-flipping experiment.

★ The big idea in the deterministic DSelect algorithm is to use the "median-of-medians" as the pivot element: break the input array into groups of 5, directly compute the median of each group, and recursively compute the median of these $\frac{n}{5}$ first-round winners.

★ The 30-70 Lemma shows that the median-of-medians guarantees a 30%-70% or better split of the input array.

★ The analysis of DSelect shows that the work spent in the recursive call to compute the median-of-medians is outweighed by the benefit of a 30%-70% split, resulting in a linear running time.

Test Your Understanding

Problem 6.1 Let α be some constant, independent of the input array length n, strictly between $\frac{1}{2}$ and 1. Suppose you are using the RSelect algorithm to compute the median element of a length-n array. What is the probability that the first recursive call is passed a subarray of length at most $\alpha \cdot n$?

a) $1 - \alpha$

b) $\alpha - \frac{1}{2}$

c) $1 - \frac{\alpha}{2}$

d) $2\alpha - 1$

Problem 6.2 Let α be some constant, independent of the input array length n, strictly between $\frac{1}{2}$ and 1. Assume that every recursive call to RSelect makes progress as in the preceding problem—so whenever a recursive call is given an array of length k, its recursive call is passed a subarray with length at most αk. What is the maximum number of successive recursive calls that can occur before triggering the base case?

a) $-\frac{\ln n}{\ln \alpha}$

b) $-\frac{\ln n}{\alpha}$

c) $-\frac{\ln n}{\ln(1-\alpha)}$

d) $-\frac{\ln n}{\ln(\frac{1}{2}+\alpha)}$

Challenge Problems

Problem 6.3 *(S)* In this problem, the input is an unsorted array of n distinct elements $x_1, x_2, \ldots, x_n$ with positive weights $w_1, w_2, \ldots, w_n$. Let W denote the sum $\sum_{i=1}^{n} w_i$ of the weights. Define a *weighted median* as an element x_k for which the total weight of all elements with value less than x_k (i.e., $\sum_{x_i < x_k} w_i$) is at most $W/2$, and also the total weight of elements with value larger than x_k (i.e., $\sum_{x_i > x_k} w_i$) is at most $W/2$. Observe that there is either one or two weighted medians.

Give a deterministic linear-time algorithm for computing a weighted median of the input array. [Hint: Use DSelect as a subroutine.]

Problem 6.4 Suppose we modify the DSelect algorithm by breaking the elements into groups of 7, rather than groups of 5. (Use the median-of-medians as the pivot element, as before.) Does this modified algorithm also run in $O(n)$ time? What if we use groups of 3?[16]

Programming Problems

Problem 6.5 Implement in your favorite programming language the RSelect algorithm from Section 6.1. Your implementation should operate in place, using an in-place implementation of Partition (which you might have implemented for Problem 5.6) and passing indices through the recursion to keep track of the still-relevant portion of the original input array. (See www.algorithmsilluminated.org for test cases and challenge data sets.)

---

[16]For a deep dive on this question, see the paper "Select with Groups of 3 or 4 Takes Linear Time," by Ke Chen and Adrian Dumitrescu (arXiv:1409.3600, 2014).

Appendix A

Quick Review of Proofs By Induction

Proofs by induction come up *all the time* in computer science. For example, in Section 5.1, we use a proof by induction to argue that the `QuickSort` algorithm always correctly sorts its input array. In Section 6.4, we use induction to prove that the `DSelect` algorithm runs in linear time.

Proofs by induction can be unintuitive, at least at first sight. The good news is that they follow a fairly rigid template, and become nearly automatic with a little practice. This appendix explains the template and provides two short examples. If you've never seen proofs by induction before, you should supplement this appendix with another source that has many more examples.[1]

A.1 A Template for Proofs by Induction

For our purposes, a proof by induction establishes an assertion $P(n)$ for every positive integer n. For example, when proving the correctness of the `QuickSort` algorithm in Section 5.1, we can define $P(n)$ as the statement: "for every input array of length n, `QuickSort` correctly sorts it." When analyzing the running time of the `DSelect` algorithm in Section 6.4, we can define $P(n)$ as "for every input array of length n, `DSelect` halts after performing at most $100n$ operations." Induction allows us to prove a property of an algorithm, like correctness or a running time bound, by establishing the property for each input length in turn.

Analogous to a recursive algorithm, a proof by induction has two parts: a *base case* and an *inductive step*. The base case proves that $P(n)$ is true for all sufficiently small values of n (typically just

---

[1]For instance, see the freely available book *Mathematics for Computer Science*, by Eric Lehman, F. Thomson Leighton, and Albert R. Meyer.

$n = 1$). In the inductive step, you assume that $P(1), \ldots, P(n-1)$ are all true and prove that $P(n)$ is consequently true as well.

Base case: Prove directly that $P(1)$ is true.

Inductive step: Prove that, for every integer $n \geq 2$,

if $\underbrace{P(1), P(2), \ldots, P(n-1) \text{ are true}}_{inductive\ hypothesis}$ then $P(n)$ is true.

In the inductive step, you get to *assume* that $P(k)$ has already been established for all values of k smaller than n—this is called the *inductive hypothesis*—and should use this assumption to establish $P(n)$.

If you prove both the base case and the inductive step, then $P(n)$ is indeed true for every positive integer n. $P(1)$ is true by the base case, and applying the inductive step over and over again shows that $P(n)$ is true for arbitrarily large values of n.

A.2   Example: A Closed-Form Formula

We can use induction to derive a closed-form formula for the sum of the first n positive integers. Let $P(n)$ denote the assertion that

$$1 + 2 + 3 + \cdots + n = \frac{(n+1)n}{2}.$$

When $n = 1$, the left-hand side is 1 and the right-hand side is $\frac{2 \cdot 1}{2} = 1$. This shows that $P(1)$ is true and completes the base case. For the inductive step, we pick an arbitrary integer $n \geq 2$ and assume that $P(1), P(2), \ldots, P(n-1)$ are all true. In particular, we can assume $P(n-1)$, which is the assertion

$$1 + 2 + 3 + \cdots + (n-1) = \frac{n(n-1)}{2}.$$

Now we can add n to both sides to derive

$$1 + 2 + 3 + \cdots + n = \frac{n(n-1)}{2} + n = \frac{n^2 - n + 2n}{2} = \frac{(n+1)n}{2},$$

which proves $P(n)$. Since we've established both the base case and the inductive step, we can conclude that $P(n)$ is true for every positive integer n.

A.3   Example: The Size of a Complete Binary Tree

Next, let's count the number of nodes in a complete binary tree with n levels. In Figure A.1, we see that with $n = 4$ levels, the number of nodes is $15 = 2^4 - 1$. Could this pattern be true in general?

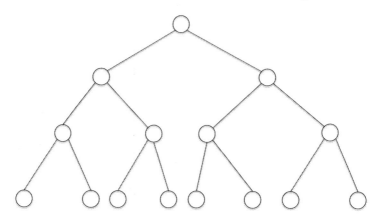

Figure A.1: A complete binary tree with 4 levels and $2^4 - 1 = 15$ nodes.

For each positive integer n, let $P(n)$ be the statement "a complete binary tree with n levels has $2^n - 1$ nodes." For the base case, note that a complete binary tree with 1 level has exactly one node. Since $2^1 - 1 = 1$, this proves that $P(1)$ is true. For the inductive step, fix a positive integer $n \geq 2$ and assume that $P(1), \ldots, P(n-1)$ are all true. The nodes of the complete binary tree with n levels can be divided into three groups: (i) the root; (ii) the nodes in the left subtree of the root; and (iii) the nodes in the right subtree of the root. The left and right subtrees of the root are themselves complete binary trees, each with $n - 1$ levels. Since we are assuming that $P(n-1)$ is true, there are exactly $2^{n-1} - 1$ nodes in each of the left and right subtrees. Adding up the nodes in the three groups, we get a total of

$$\underbrace{1}_{\text{root}} + \underbrace{2^{n-1} - 1}_{\text{left subtree}} + \underbrace{2^{n-1} - 1}_{\text{right subtree}} = 2^n - 1$$

nodes in the tree. This proves the statement $P(n)$ and, since $n \geq 2$ was arbitrary, completes the inductive step. We conclude that $P(n)$ is true for every positive integer n.

Appendix B

Quick Review of Discrete Probability

This appendix reviews the concepts from discrete probability that are necessary for our analysis of randomized `QuickSort` (Theorem 5.1 and Section 5.5): sample spaces, events, random variables, expectation, and linearity of expectation. Section B.6 concludes with a load-balancing example that ties all these concepts together. We will also use these concepts in future parts of this book series, in the contexts of data structures, graph algorithms, and local search algorithms. If you're seeing this material for the first time, you probably want to supplement this appendix with a more thorough treatment.[1] If you have seen it before, don't feel compelled to read this appendix from front to back—dip in as needed wherever you need a refresher.

B.1   Sample Spaces

We're interested in random processes, in which any number of different things might happen. The *sample space* is the set Ω of all the different things that could happen—the universe in which we're going to assign probabilities, take average values, and so on. For example, if our random process is the throw of a six-sided die, then $\Omega = \{1, 2, 3, 4, 5, 6\}$. Happily, in the analysis of randomized algorithms, we can almost always take Ω to be a finite set and work only with discrete probability, which is much more elementary than general probability theory.

Each element i of a sample space Ω comes with a nonnegative *probability* $p(i)$, which can be thought of as the frequency with which the outcome of the random process is i. For example, if a six-sided die is fair, then $p(i)$ is $\frac{1}{6}$ for each $i = 1, 2, 3, 4, 5, 6$. In general, since Ω is supposed to be everything that could possibly happen, the

---

[1]For example, there is a free Wikibook on discrete probability (`https://en.wikibooks.org/wiki/High_School_Mathematics_Extensions/Discrete_Probability`).

probabilities should sum to 1:

$$\sum_{i \in \Omega} p(i) = 1.$$

A common special case is when every element of Ω is equally likely—known as the *uniform distribution*—in which case $p(i) = \frac{1}{|\Omega|}$ for every $i \in \Omega$.[2] This may seem like a pretty abstract concept, so let's introduce two running examples. In the first example, the random process is a throw of two standard (six-sided) dice. The sample space is the set of 36 different things that could happen:

$$\Omega = \underbrace{\{(1,1),(2,1),(3,1),\ldots,(5,6),(6,6)\}}_{\text{36 ordered pairs}}.$$

Assuming the dice are fair, each of these outcomes is equally likely: $p(i) = \frac{1}{36}$ for every $i \in \Omega$.

The second example, more germane to algorithms, is the choice of the pivot element in the outermost call to randomized `QuickSort` (Section 5.4). Any element of the input array can be chosen as the pivot, so

$$\Omega = \underbrace{\{1,2,3,\ldots,n\}}_{\text{possible positions of pivot element}} ,$$

where n is the length of the input array. By definition, in randomized `QuickSort` each element is equally likely to be chosen as the pivot element, and so $p(i) = \frac{1}{n}$ for every $i \in \Omega$.

B.2   Events

An *event* is a subset $S \subseteq \Omega$ of the sample space—a collection of possible outcomes of a random process. The probability $\mathbf{Pr}[S]$ of an event S is defined as you would expect, as the probability that one of the outcomes of S occurs:

$$\mathbf{Pr}[S] = \sum_{i \in S} p(i).$$

Let's get some practice with this concept using our two running examples.

---

[2]For a finite set S, $|S|$ denotes the number of elements in S.

Quiz B.1

Let S denote the set of outcomes for which the sum of two standard dice equals 7. What is the probability of the event S?[3]

  a) $\frac{1}{36}$

  b) $\frac{1}{12}$

  c) $\frac{1}{6}$

  d) $\frac{1}{2}$

(See Section B.2.1 for the solution and discussion.)

The second quiz concerns the choice of the random pivot element in the outermost call to QuickSort. We say that a pivot element is an "approximate median" if at least 25% of the array elements are less than the pivot, and at least 25% of the elements are greater than the pivot.

Quiz B.2

Let S denote the event that the chosen pivot element in the outermost call to QuickSort is an approximate median. What is the probability of the event S?

  a) $\frac{1}{n}$, where n is the length of the array

  b) $\frac{1}{4}$

  c) $\frac{1}{2}$

  d) $\frac{3}{4}$

(See Section B.2.2 for the solution and discussion.)

---

[3] A useful fact to know when playing the dice game craps...

B.2.1   Solution to Quiz B.1

Correct answer: (c). There are six outcomes in which the sum of
the two dice equals 7:

$$S = \{(6,1), (5,2), (4,3), (3,4), (2,5), (1,6)\}.$$

Since every outcome of Ω is equally likely, $p(i) = \frac{1}{36}$ for every $i \in S$
and so
$$\mathbf{Pr}[S] = |S| \cdot \tfrac{1}{36} = \tfrac{6}{36} = \tfrac{1}{6}.$$

B.2.2   Solution to Quiz B.2

Correct answer: (c). As a thought experiment, imagine dividing
the elements in the input array into four groups: the smallest $\frac{n}{4}$
elements, the next-smallest $\frac{n}{4}$ elements, the next-smallest $\frac{n}{4}$ elements,
and finally the largest $\frac{n}{4}$ elements. (As usual, we're ignoring fractions
for simplicity.) Every element of the second and third groups is an
approximate median: all the $\frac{n}{4}$ elements from the first and last groups
are less than and greater than the pivot, respectively. Conversely, if
the algorithm picks a pivot element from either the first or the last
group, either the elements less than the pivot comprise only a strict
subset of the first group, or the elements greater than the pivot are
only a strict subset of the last group. In this case, the pivot element is
not an approximate median. Thus the event S corresponds to the $\frac{n}{2}$
elements in the second and third groups; since each element is equally
likely to be chosen as the pivot element,

$$\mathbf{Pr}[S] = |S| \cdot \tfrac{1}{n} = \tfrac{n}{2} \cdot \tfrac{1}{n} = \tfrac{1}{2}.$$

B.3   Random Variables

A *random variable* is a numerical measurement of the outcome of a
random process. Formally, it is a real-valued function $X : \Omega \to \mathbb{R}$
defined on the sample space Ω—the input $i \in \Omega$ to X is an outcome
of the random process, and the output $X(i)$ is a numerical value.

In our first running example, we can define a random variable
that is the sum of the two dice. This random variable maps outcomes
(pairs (i, j) with $i, j \in \{1, 2, \ldots, 6\}$) to real numbers according to the

map $(i, j) \mapsto i + j$. In our second running example, we can define a random variable that is the length of the subarray passed to the first recursive call to QuickSort. This random variable maps each outcome (that is, each choice of a pivot element) to an integer between 0 (if the chosen pivot is the minimum element) and $n - 1$, where n is the length of the input array (if the chosen pivot is the maximum element).

Section 5.5 studies the random variable X that is the running time of randomized QuickSort on a given input array. Here, the state space Ω is all possible sequences of pivot elements the algorithm might choose, and $X(i)$ is the number of operations performed by the algorithm for a particular sequence $i \in \Omega$ of pivot choices.[4]

B.4   Expectation

The *expectation* or *expected value* $\mathbf{E}[X]$ of a random variable X is its average value over everything that could happen, weighted appropriately with the probabilities of different outcomes. Intuitively, if a random process is repeated over and over again, $\mathbf{E}[X]$ is the long-run average value of the random variable X. For example, if X is the value of a fair six-sided die, then $\mathbf{E}[X] = 3.5$.

In math, if $X : \Omega \to \mathbb{R}$ is a random variable and $p(i)$ denotes the probability of outcome $i \in \Omega$,

$$\mathbf{E}[X] = \sum_{i \in \Omega} p(i) \cdot X(i). \tag{B.1}$$

The next two quizzes ask you to compute the expectation of the two random variables defined in the preceding section.

Quiz B.3

What is the expectation of the sum of two dice?

a) 6.5

b) 7

c) 7.5

---

[4]Since the only randomness in randomized QuickSort is in the choice of pivot elements, once we fix these choices, QuickSort has some well-defined running time.

d) 8

(See Section B.4.1 for the solution and discussion.)

Returning to randomized `QuickSort`, how big, on average, is the length of the subarray passed to the first recursive call? Equivalently, how many elements are less than a randomly chosen pivot on average?

Quiz B.4

Which of the following is closest to the expectation of the size of the subarray passed to the first recursive call in `QuickSort`?

a) $\frac{n}{4}$

b) $\frac{n}{3}$

c) $\frac{n}{2}$

d) $\frac{3n}{4}$

(See Section B.4.2 for the solution and discussion.)

B.4.1   Solution to Quiz B.3

Correct answer: (b). There are several ways to see why the expectation is 7. The first way is to compute it by brute force, using the defining equation (B.1). With 36 possible outcomes, this is doable but tedious. A slicker way is to pair up the possible values of the sum and use symmetry. The sum is equally likely to be 2 or 12, equally likely to be 3 or 11, and so on. In each of these pairs the average value is 7, so this is also the average value overall. The third and best way is to use linearity of expectation, as covered in the next section.

B.4.2   Solution to Quiz B.4

Correct answer: (c). The exact value of the expectation is $(n-1)/2$. There is a $1/n$ chance that the subarray has length 0 (if the pivot element is the smallest element), a $1/n$ chance that it has length 1 (if the pivot element is the second-smallest element), and so on, up to a $1/n$ chance that it has length $n-1$ (if the pivot element is the largest element). By the definition (B.1) of expectation, and recalling the identity $\sum_{i=1}^{n-1} i = \frac{n(n-1)}{2}$,[5] we have

$$\mathbf{E}[X] = \frac{1}{n} \cdot 0 + \frac{1}{n} \cdot 1 + \cdots + \frac{1}{n} \cdot (n-1) = \frac{1}{n} \cdot \underbrace{(1 + 2 + \cdots + (n-1))}_{=\frac{n(n-1)}{2}}$$

$$= \frac{n-1}{2}.$$

B.5 Linearity of Expectation

B.5.1 Formal Statement and Use Cases

Our final concept is a mathematical property, not a definition. *Linearity of expectation* is the property that the expectation of a sum of random variables is equal to the sum of their individual expectations. It is incredibly useful for computing the expectation of a complex random variable, like the running time of randomized `QuickSort`, when the random variable can be expressed as a weighted sum of simpler random variables.

Theorem B.1 (Linearity of Expectation) *Let* $X_1, \ldots, X_n$ *be random variables defined on the same sample space* Ω, *and let* $a_1, \ldots, a_n$ *be real numbers. Then*

$$\mathbf{E}\left[\sum_{j=1}^{n} a_j \cdot X_j\right] = \sum_{j=1}^{n} a_j \cdot \mathbf{E}[X_j]. \tag{B.2}$$

That is, you can take the sum and the expectation in either order and get the same thing. The common use case is when $\sum_{j=1}^{n} a_j X_j$ is a complex random variable (like the running time of randomized

---

[5]One way to see that $1 + 2 + \cdots + (n-1) = \frac{n(n-1)}{2}$ is to use induction on n (see Section A.2). For a sneakier proof, take two copies of the left-hand side and pair up the "1" from the first copy with the "$n-1$" from the second copy, the "2" from the first copy with the "$n-2$" from the second copy, and so on. This gives $n-1$ pairs with value n each. Since double the sum equals $n(n-1)$, the original sum equals $\frac{n(n-1)}{2}$.

`QuickSort`) and the X_j's are simple random variables (like 0-1 random variables).[6]

For example, let X be the sum of two standard dice. We can write X as the sum of two random variables X_1 and X_2, which are the values of the first and second die, respectively. The expectation of X_1 or X_2 is easy to compute using the definition (B.1) as $\frac{1}{6}(1+2+3+4+5+6) = 3.5$. Linearity of expectation then gives

$$\mathbf{E}[X] = \mathbf{E}[X_1] + \mathbf{E}[X_2] = 3.5 + 3.5 = 7,$$

replicating our answer in Section B.4.1 with less work.

An extremely important point is that *linearity of expectation holds even for random variables that are not independent.* We won't need to formally define independence in this book, but you probably have good intuition about what it means: knowing something about the value of one random variable doesn't tell you anything new about the values of the others. For example, the random variables X_1 and X_2 above are independent because the two dice are assumed to be thrown independently.

For an example of dependent random variables, consider a pair of magnetically linked dice, where the second die always comes up with value one larger than that of the first (or 1, if the first die comes up 6). Now, knowing the value of either die tells you exactly what the value of the other die is. But we can still write the sum X of the two dice as $X_1 + X_2$, where X_1 and X_2 are the values of the two dice. It is still the case that X_1, viewed in isolation, is equally likely to be each of $\{1, 2, 3, 4, 5, 6\}$, and the same is true for X_2. Thus we still have $\mathbf{E}[X_1] = \mathbf{E}[X_2] = 3.5$ and by linearity of expectation we still have $\mathbf{E}[X] = 7$.

Why should you be surprised? Superficially, the identity in (B.2) might look like a tautology. But if we switch from sums to *products* of random variables, the analog of Theorem B.1 no longer holds for dependent random variables.[7] So linearity of expectation really is a special property about sums of random variables.

---

[6]In the Stanford version of this course, over ten weeks of blackboard lectures, I draw a box around exactly one mathematical identity—linearity of expectation.

[7]The magnetically linked dice provide one counterexample. For an even simpler counterexample, suppose X_1 and X_2 are either equal to 0 and 1, or to 1 and 0, with each outcome having 50% probability. Then $\mathbf{E}[X_1 \cdot X_2] = 0$ while $\mathbf{E}[X_1] \cdot \mathbf{E}[X_2] = \frac{1}{4}$.

B.5.2   The Proof

The utility of linearity of expectation is matched only by the simplicity of its proof.[8]

Proof of Theorem B.1: Starting with the right-hand side of (B.2) and expanding using the definition (B.1) of expectation gives

$$\sum_{j=1}^{n} a_j \cdot \mathbf{E}[X_j] = \sum_{j=1}^{n} a_j \cdot \left(\sum_{i \in \Omega} p(i) \cdot X_j(i) \right)$$

$$= \sum_{j=1}^{n} \left(\sum_{i \in \Omega} a_j \cdot p(i) \cdot X_j(i) \right).$$

Reversing the order of summation, we have

$$\sum_{j=1}^{n} \left(\sum_{i \in \Omega} a_j \cdot p(i) \cdot X_j(i) \right) = \sum_{i \in \Omega} \left(\sum_{j=1}^{n} a_j \cdot p(i) \cdot X_j(i) \right). \quad \text{(B.3)}$$

Since $p(i)$ is independent of $j = 1, 2, \ldots, n$, we can pull it out of the inner sum:

$$\sum_{i \in \Omega} \left(\sum_{j=1}^{n} a_j \cdot p(i) \cdot X_j(i) \right) = \sum_{i \in \Omega} p(i) \cdot \left(\sum_{j=1}^{n} a_j \cdot X_j(i) \right).$$

Finally, using again the definition (B.1) of expectation, we obtain the left-hand side of (B.2):

$$\sum_{i \in \Omega} p(i) \cdot \left(\sum_{j=1}^{n} a_j \cdot X_j(i) \right) = \mathbf{E}\left[\sum_{j=1}^{n} a_j \cdot X_j \right].$$

QED

That's it! Linearity of expectation is really just a reversal of a double summation.

Speaking of double summations, equation (B.3) might seem opaque if you're rusty on these kinds of algebraic manipulations. For a down-to-earth way to think about it, arrange the $a_j p(i) X_j(i)$'s in a grid,

---

[8]The first time you read this proof, you should assume for simplicity that $a_1 = a_2 = \cdots = a_n = 1$.

with rows indexed by $i \in \Omega$, columns indexed by $j \in \{1, 2, \ldots, n\}$, and the number $a_j \cdot p(i) \cdot X_j(i)$ in the cell in the ith row and jth column:

$$\left\{ \begin{array}{c} \uparrow \\ i \\ \downarrow \end{array} \right. \quad \boxed{\begin{array}{cccc} \ddots & \vdots & & \\ & \vdots & & \\ \cdots \quad \cdots & a_j p(i) X_j(i) & \cdots & \cdots \\ & \vdots & & \\ & \vdots & & \ddots \end{array}}$$

$$\longleftarrow j \longrightarrow$$

The left-hand side of (B.3) first sums up each of the columns, and then adds up these column sums. The right-hand side first sums up the rows and then sums up these row sums. Either way, you get the sum of all the entries in the grid.

B.6   Example: Load Balancing

To tie together all the preceding concepts, let's study an example about load balancing. Suppose we need an algorithm that assigns processes to servers, but we're feeling super-lazy. One easy solution is to just assign each process to a random server, with each server equally likely. How well does this work?[9]

For concreteness, assume there are n processes and also n servers, where n is some positive integer. First, let's be clear on the sample space: the set Ω is all n^n possible ways of assigning the processes to the servers, with n choices for each of the n processes. By the definition of our lazy algorithm, each of these n^n outcomes is equally likely.

Now that we have a sample space, we're in a position to define random variables. One interesting quantity is server load, so let's define Y as the random variable equal to the number of processes that get assigned to the first server. (The story is the same for all the servers by symmetry, so we may as well focus on the first one.) What is the expectation of Y?

In principle, we can compute $\mathbf{E}[Y]$ by brute-force evaluation of the defining equation (B.1), but this is impractical for all but the

---

[9]This example is also relevant to our discussion of hashing in *Part 2*.

smallest values of n. Fortunately, since Y can be expressed as a sum of simple random variables, linearity of expectation can save the day. Formally, for $j = 1, 2, \ldots, n$, define

$$X_j = \begin{cases} 1 & \text{if the } j\text{th process gets assigned to the first server} \\ 0 & \text{otherwise.} \end{cases}$$

Random variables that only take on the values 0 and 1 are often called *indicator* random variables because they indicate whether some event occurs (like the event that process j gets assigned to the first server). From the definitions, we can express Y as the sum of the X_j's:

$$Y = \sum_{j=1}^{n} X_j.$$

By linearity of expectation (Theorem B.1), the expectation of Y is then the sum of the expectations of the X_j's:

$$\mathbf{E}[Y] = \mathbf{E}\left[\sum_{j=1}^{n} X_j\right] = \sum_{j=1}^{n} \mathbf{E}[X_j].$$

Because each random variable X_j is so simple, it's easy to compute its expectation directly:

$$\mathbf{E}[X_j] = \underbrace{0 \cdot \mathbf{Pr}[X_j = 0]}_{=0} + 1 \cdot \mathbf{Pr}[X_j = 1] = \mathbf{Pr}[X_j = 1].$$

Since the jth process is equally likely to be assigned to each of the n servers, $\mathbf{Pr}[X_j = 1] = \frac{1}{n}$. Putting it all together, we have

$$\mathbf{E}[Y] = \sum_{j=1}^{n} \mathbf{E}[X_j] = n \cdot \frac{1}{n} = 1.$$

So if we care only about average server loads, our super-lazy algorithm works just fine! This example and randomized `QuickSort` are characteristic of the role that randomization plays in algorithm design: we can often get away with really simple heuristics if we make random choices along the way.

Quiz B.5

Consider a group of k people. Assume that each person's birthday is drawn uniformly at random from the 365 possibilities. (And ignore leap years.) What is the smallest value of k such that the expected number of pairs of distinct people with the same birthday is at least one? [Hint: Define an indicator random variable for each pair of people. Use linearity of expectation.]

 a) 20

 b) 23

 c) 27

 d) 28

 e) 366

(See below for the solution and discussion.)

Correct answer: (d). Fix a positive integer k, and denote the set of people by $\{1, 2, \ldots, k\}$. Let Y denote the number of pairs of people with the same birthday. As suggested by the hint, define one random variable X_{ij} for every choice $i, j \in \{1, 2, \ldots, k\}$ of people with $i < j$. Define X_{ij} as 1 if i and j have the same birthday and 0 otherwise. Thus, the X_{ij}'s are indicator random variables, and

$$Y = \sum_{i=1}^{k-1} \sum_{j=i+1}^{k} X_{ij}.$$

By linearity of expectation (Theorem B.1),

$$\mathbf{E}[Y] = \mathbf{E}\left[\sum_{i=1}^{k-1} \sum_{j=i+1}^{k} X_{ij}\right] = \sum_{i=1}^{k-1} \sum_{j=i+1}^{k} \mathbf{E}[X_{ij}]. \qquad (\text{B.4})$$

Since X_{ij} is an indicator random variable, $\mathbf{E}[X_{ij}] = \mathbf{Pr}[X_{ij} = 1]$. There are $(365)^2$ possibilities for the birthdays of the people i and j, and in 365 of these possibilities i and j have the same birthday.

Assuming that all birthday combinations are equally likely,

$$\mathbf{Pr}[X_{ij} = 1] = \frac{365}{(365)^2} = \frac{1}{365}.$$

Plugging this in to (B.4), we have

$$\mathbf{E}[Y] = \sum_{i=1}^{k-1} \sum_{j=i+1}^{k} \frac{1}{365} = \frac{1}{365} \cdot \binom{k}{2} = \frac{k(k-1)}{730},$$

where $\binom{k}{2}$ denotes the binomial coefficient "k choose 2" (as in the solution to Quiz 3.1). The smallest value of k for which $k(k-1)/730 \geq 1$ is 28.

Solutions to Selected Problems

Problem 1.1: The "2" is in the 7th position.

Problem 1.4: (c). There are $\approx \log_2 k$ iterations and each iteration takes time proportional to nk.

Problem 2.1: (a). Because the constant c in the exponent is inside a logarithm, it becomes part of the leading constant and gets suppressed in the big-O notation.

Problem 2.5: Exponentiation base-2 and the logarithm base-2 are inverse operations, so $2^{\log_2 n}$ is the same as n and $2^{2^{\log_2 n}}$ is the same as 2^n. Thus the correct ordering is (a), (e), (c), (b), (d).

Problem 3.2: The algorithm is similar to binary search. It first examines the middle element and the elements on either side. If the middle element is bigger than both its neighbors, then it is the maximum element (because the array is unimodal). Otherwise the algorithm recurses on whichever side of the array contains the larger neighbor. In the notation of the master method, $a = 1$, $b = 2$, and $d = 0$, so the running time is $O(\log n)$ (by case 1).

Problem 3.3: A variation on binary search solves the problem in $O(\log n)$ time. If the input array is empty, answer "no." Otherwise, check the middle element and compare its value $A[i]$ to its position i in the array. If they're the same number, answer "yes;" otherwise, recurse on either the left side of the array (if $A[i] > i$) or the right side (if $A[i] < i$).

Problem 4.1: (d). See page 107.

Problem 4.2: (b). In the notation of the master method, $a = 7$, $b = 3$, and $d = 2$; using case 2, $T(n) = O(n^2)$.

Problem 4.5: (b). Write n as $2^{\log_2 n}$. Each application of T cuts the exponent in half. The exponent drops from $\log_2 n$ to 1 in $\approx \log_2 \log_2 n$ iterations, so $T(n) = O(\log \log n)$.

Problem 5.1: The answer is every number that is bigger than everything to the left of it and smaller than everything to the right of it: 4, 5, and 9.

Problem 5.4: (b). In the best-case scenario, the algorithm always picks the median as the pivot element. In this case, the recursion tree is essentially identical to that of `MergeSort`, which has logarithmic depth. In the worst-case scenario, the algorithm always picks the minimum or maximum element as the pivot, in which case the recursion depth is linear.

Problem 6.3: Compute the total weight W (in linear time). Initialize D_L and D_R to 0; these variables will track the total weight of discarded elements that are less than and greater than the elements of the current subarray, respectively. In the outermost recursive call, use `DSelect` to compute the (unweighted) median and `Partition` to partition the array around it (all in linear time). If the total weight on each side of the median is at most $W/2$, return it. Otherwise, recurse on the (unique) half of the array with total weight more than $W/2$, updating D_L or D_R to keep track of the total weight of the discarded elements.

In a general recursive call, use `DSelect` to compute the (unweighted) median of the remaining subarray, `Partition` the subarray around this median, and compute the total weight W_L and W_R of the subarray elements on each side. If both $W_L + D_L$ and $W_R + D_R$ are at most $W/2$, return this median (it is a weighted median of the original input array, as you should check). Otherwise, recurse on the (unique) half of the subarray with $W_L + D_L$ or $W_R + D_R$ greater than $W/2$, updating D_L or D_R accordingly.

The algorithm's running time is governed by the recurrence $T(n) \leq T(n/2) + O(n)$. By case 2 of the master method, $T(n) = O(n)$ and so the algorithm runs in linear time.

Index

Made in the USA
Middletown, DE
10 October 2020